A Poet's Bible

A POET'S BIBLE

REDISCOVERING

THE VOICES OF

THE ORIGINAL TEXT

David Rosenberg

HYPERION

NEW YORK

Library of Congress Cataloging-in-Publication Data
Rosenberg, David
A poet's bible : rediscovering the voices of the original text/
David Rosenberg.
p.   cm.
ISBN 1-56282-922-X
1. Bible. O.T.—History of Biblical events—Poetry.   2. Jewish
religious poetry, American.   I. Title.
PS3568.0783P6   1993
811'.54—dc20   92-32849
CIP

FIRST PAPERBACK EDITION
10 9 8 7 6 5 4 3 2 1

*To the memory
of Herman Rosenberg
my father*

*"The best way to see stars
is to look a little to one side"*
—James Schuyler

ACKNOWLEDGMENTS

A Poet's Bible *required ten years' labor to allow the chorus of writers behind the text to step forward—to my ear—and separate into discrete individuals. More recently, some of the works in* A Poet's Bible *have been revised from earlier versions; Lewis Warsh, Clayton Carlson, Randall Greene, and Seymour Barofsky were instrumental to the first attempts. Lew Grimes, of the Grimes Agency, took this book under wing; Robert Miller and Jenny Cox of Hyperion added sure vision and sensitive editing. Some others whose personal words were essential: Harold Schimmel, Michal Govrin, Dennis Silk, Bill Zavatsky, Harvey Shapiro, Martin Peretz, Donald Hall, David Shapiro, Grace Schulman, Walter Brown, Marina Tamar Budhos, Jody Leopold, Helen Mitsios, and the late Wolfe Kelman. Finally, I'm grateful to The Writer's Room in New York and Mishkenot Sha'ananim in Jerusalem.*

CONTENTS

INTRODUCTION

THE BIBLE AS POETRY

Unconventional Poets

The Bible, arguably the most important work of art in the Western
literary canon, is an uneasy subject in the classroom. Why are our
great poetic stories taught in the dullest of ways? I believe the fault
can be traced to a failure of imagination in academic life. Imagina-
tion can be stifled by dogma, but it can also be flattened by theories
that handle merely the skeletons of texts. The Bible is a luminous
guidebook to our past yet it is put out of reach by colorless profes-
sors. And the broad range of poets who gave voice to the original
words have been rendered voiceless by prosaic translations. Once,
the poets lent us what one critic has called, in the context of soul
music, the "spiritual magnitude of the individual voice." It is time
to rediscover the original text.

•   •   •

Many brilliant men and women wrote the Hebrew Bible and
Apocrypha during a period of ten centuries, building upon the
example of the original *J* writer, who, scholars suppose, wrote the
first strand in *Genesis, Exodus,* and *Numbers,* probably in the tenth
century B.C. (Scholarly initials have referred to the Bible's original
writers for more than a century in biblical criticism: *J* is also called
the Jahwist, or Yahwist, *P* the priestly writer, *E* the Elohist, and,
among others, *S* is the court historian who wrote the stories of
David and Solomon.) Finally, the images of Moses as God's secre-
tary or of countless "religious scribes" are being replaced by an
emerging picture of our genuine ancestral authors.

Modern scholarship and archaeology allow us insights into
ancient life, and by comparing the cultures and languages of other
kingdoms of the period we can conceive of the Bible's authors as

professional poets from the educated classes, schooled in languages and world literature—and not predominantly religious in outlook. They lived in a Hebraic culture quite distinct from what we call Judaism today, though strong links remain. Even the biblical text reminds us they were esteemed individuals in their own day; some of their names survive in the verses, like Asaph, Baruch, and the nickname Qohelet. To restore their human dimension, we need to rediscover them as vital, sexual human beings like ourselves. Among the women writers (who inherited a tradition of creative women dating back to Deborah, Abigail, and Hulda), some may have been widows and orphans, as well as sisters, wives, and daughters of the elite classes—even during times when custom circumscribed the sexes in the general population.

Few of us were inspired to discover these original poets in Bible classes. In effect, the authorship of the Bible continues to be suppressed. Why does it seem to be so difficult for religion to discover the humanity of a great classical culture? I believe the answer is weak faith and weaker imagination. The powerful Hebraic culture in which religion found a way to speak has also been repressed. Can we imagine a rabbi, priest, or professor of religion having authored such subtle and ironic poetic texts as *Jonah* or *Ruth?* Do we know of any religious writers who could equal the poetry in *Psalms* or *Isaiah?* As we reclaim the voices of these writers, a new vision of the origins of Western culture emerges to refresh the spirit—and revise our ideas of how to learn from the past.

•   •   •

The Hebrew poets of the Bible are more like our writers today than the conventional religious stereotypes. The representations of God among the biblical poets varied as much as it still does among modern writers, and several books—from *Ecclesiastes* to *Esther* to *Judith*—are almost indifferent to God or religion. These books and parts of many others make up an imaginative literature greater than the Hebrew Bible itself, including the Apocrypha and other noncanonical works. *Psalms, Isaiah,* the books of the other prophets, and *Job* and *Jonah* are among those abundant with differing visions of God. The poets who wrote these books constitute only a fraction of a great culture of writers—poets of primarily literary texts—many of whose works have been lost along with their names.

. . .

To discover the living voices of the poets—three thousand years old, in some cases—I needed to reimagine myself as a writer determined and bound by culture, grappling for freedom from convention. The mandates of conventional religion exist in any age; for the earliest and latest biblical poets, the impinging religion might have been pagan; today, it is just as likely to be Judeo-Christian. The biblical prophets are the most famous examples of poets who resisted the prevailing conventions.

All the Bible's poets question the habits of their audience in quietly provocative ways. Just as yesterday's cutting edge can today be pedestrian—and yesterday's convention can already be no longer habitual—I want to keep in mind what a Hebrew poet was up against. Readers would have been moved only by the power of their own sentiments, and not by the writer's vision, if the poet merely followed custom. Instead, he stays one step ahead of the reader: where a cliché is expected, it is broken, and where grandiosity is expected, something familiar and simple pops up. And even a cliché, when unexpected, can come back to life.

To imagine any biblical poet as human—to make him or her personal—I have to consider what conventions he is called to struggle against. To do this, I myself have to break with scholarly convention and consider the limitations of my own personal history, particularly because the Bible permeates so many levels of our culture. Many scholars shrink from this, sometimes out of fear of exposure, sometimes because they fear a kind of self-witnessing that resembles a confession of faith. And yet such a faith is necessary for a poet—it's his calling, basic to the bond between reader and writer. It's a reaching, for sure—a need to reach out. There is certainly helplessness in it, and grandiosity as well; the mixture may differ in writers and in ages, but the formula remains the same.

It helps to remember how personal the early poets of the Bible could be, using God's names in familiar, often punning ways; the convention of substituting "Lord" or "God" for the deity came later. The poets of the European Renaissance adopted a similar, high-minded playfulness toward their patrons and muses. The poet of *Jonah* even caricatured her own dependence on a patronlike God. It's in the textual irony of *Jonah* that I begin to hear the author's voice as a woman's, as she attempts to override the masculine clichés of prophecy. True poetry unfolds the author's presence, male or female, as an artistic force and not a passive vehicle for doctrine. I will explain why one of the authors of *Lamentations* was probably a woman, as were the authors of *Judith* and *Jonah,* while the author of the *Song of Solomon* was a man—and most likely the original King Solomon himself (though a woman very likely collaborated with him).

Conventional religion emphasized patriarchal views, and so have conventional scholars, who tend to dwell on rules they find in the text. A poet, on the other hand, is moved by the original author's creativity, and in the Bible that art almost always appears unconventional, especially after the narrow ways we've been taught to read it.

The Poet's Voice

When I became an adolescent poet I was not so much writing poetry as translating a memory of poetry, of how I heard the Hebrew psalms in childhood: a speaking to God, chanted gently as if God liked rhyme and lullaby—as if He were my parents' fathers and He was singing through them. I can remember standing no higher than my father's prayer shawl fringes, watching him sing the psalms to himself in synagogue. I continue to think of poems as translations—even translations of a child's cries, just as the Bible's psalms will often cry out to mother and father, in between the murmuring and chanting.

Those cries of the inner child are a poet's proof that the unconscious is being heard. Poetry is often about rediscovering an original voice. This first voice remains within, never discarded but slowly growing anonymous, until we don't hear ourselves in it. As a child sitting beside my father in synagogue, did I want to know what the anonymous Hebrew text meant? No, I just wanted to be next to my father, even as I began counting the lightbulbs in the chandeliers.

I was glad *he* was doing the praying because I didn't want to. Yet as long he participated, I felt part of the team. God was part of that team also—the head of it, perhaps. God in a way was like my mother, an invisible presence (free to stay home), also like Dad's father and mother, whose names were on on a brass plate on the huge wall of the deceased, a tiny light bulb beside each family name. The little bulbs burned throughout the week on which a family deathday was remembered. I loved those lights and loved reading the names beside them; my desire was for connection, continuity. As I grew older and the biblical words grew plainer before my eyes, the Hebrew texts themselves connected me to all the family names extending into the past.

Are they texts or are they voices? The first voice I discovered in them was my own: If I could have written this psalm, I told myself as a young poet, I would be deeply satisfied. Later, the voice within the text emerged, but only after I learned to distinguish the literary voice from the author's intentions. How can I know the author's intentions? I can only imagine them. But if I fail to imagine them, I miss a deep continuity preserved by great, ancient poetry. Our science has improved, yet today I can still put aside pretenses of progress when I hear the personal speech of the past. If you don't read poetry, an impersonal, incantatory utterance— the chanting I first heard in the synagogue—may be enough. For myself, I had to discover the many human voices behind the liturgy. I had to hear the original poems.

The Call

I was drawn to reconsider the nature of inspiration as I worked on *A Poet's Bible.* I realized that we are indoctrinated against imagining the relationship between biblical verse and contemporary poetry. Since a mere vehicle of a man, or a didactic writer, could hardly have created the vivid masterpieces in the Bible, the conviction grew in me that biblical poets nourished a sense of awe toward literary talent that resembles our own. When their artistic calling is obscured, the playfulness in the text seems to disappear, along with the creative modes that produce irony, humor, anguish, and ambiguity.

After focusing on imagining the authors, I considered the sources from which their inspiration flowed. I began to recognize that in each case the original author answered a *call,* just as a modern poet does: sometimes it was a call from the body, the senses; sometimes it was an inner summons, as in a dream or meditation; and other times it was summoned up for the sake of telling a story. I respond to a call by interpreting it, and this leads me to ask crucial questions about unknown writers and their work: Why were *Ruth* and *Esther* written? What was at the core of these stories, calling for the author's response? What are they stories *about?* Women? Survival? Since the knowledge we have about the biblical authors comes from their texts, I had to reimagine them— not as religious men and women, but as well-practiced poets. These ancient Hebrew poets are simply too eloquent to be dismissed as writers of preachy works.

When I divided *A Poet's Bible* in three—the bodily senses, the intuition, and the intellect—I recognized the correspondence between what we call psychology and what the ancient poets knew as states of being. The Hebrew Bible is also divided into three parts: the first, the Pentateuch, is primary, like a body (it is sometimes imagined as such in tradition, and even the Torah scroll has a crown placed on its head); the second, the Prophets, is a socialization of the body; and the third, the Writings, projects this body into the wide world.

Many years after the death of the *J* writer, who wrote the Pentateuch's original strand, she was forgotten as a human being. But centuries later, the poets who continued to write the works of prophecy, story, lyric, and lament that make up the Hebrew Bible, drew upon the wit of her creation. Just as the writers of the New Testament relied upon the Hebrew poets, so the Hebrew poets also depended on the *J* and *S* writers, whose God is portrayed with uncanny wit. Using the powerful wordplay in *J*'s lines, the biblical poets elaborated on the ancient rules of form called parallelism until they produced a spontaneous art. Parallelism stands for subtle uses of repetition in all aspects of language, and we've grown increasingly insensitive to it as poetry has fallen away from a conscious part of the mainstream.

The significance of the biblical poet's calling lay in shaping our consciousness of language, but today the poet's mission is overshadowed by popular culture. Even the standard textbook in English, *The Bible as Literature*, has to reach for music metaphors to describe biblical poetry. Parallelism, we learn, is like "traditional jazz, where the unvarying four-square beat on which the music is built may never come to the surface as such and where the art of the performers seems often to be gauged by the extent to which they can depart from this beat without ever forgetting their way back to it." But can a reader experience this heady jazz on paper? Conventional wisdom keeps us from conceiving that the best of the Bible's great poets were virtuosos as renowned in their day as Louis Armstrong—or James Joyce, among wordsmiths—is in ours.

The extremely pious, who believe that no down-to-earth humans were involved in writing the Bible, may understandably refuse to consider the identity of the original authors. But what about the new generation of academic teachers and religious scholars? Why are they often unprepared—compared with teachers of Homer, for instance—to imagine what a living poet thinks and feels? If the poet's calling, or inspiration, is a sacred mystery, and great literature doesn't require years of practice to give it shape, then these teachers are safe from having to consider authorship.

Yet they've lost touch with the essence of poetry: the great poet's individuality, his struggle with self-awareness, even when his name is discounted.

Translating the Bible

What is less in error, a leaden cliché in place of the vibrant, ancient image, or an energetic, contemporary image that parallels the original Hebrew? Preferring the latter, I believe that the official translations of the Bible today are imaginatively inaccurate, their diction and idiom unfaithful to the spirit of the original. I want to hear accurate parallels for the ancient Hebrew idiom, a level of translation that makes the Hebrew resonate.

Jewish tradition has always avoided literal translation, and post-biblical writers wove entire parallel stories out of the biblical text, furthering a creative culture. Midrash (imaginative interpretation) became a normative mode of translation for communities in later ages. In this poetic tradition, my work could be called interpretive translation, since it keeps close to the original Hebrew.

Standard translations into English have followed a traditional practice of erasing the original authors' voices. It isn't easy to know where this tradition began but if we look back we can find a counter-tradition. During ancient Israel's second kingdom, the Hebrew Bible was read in Aramaic translations called Targumim, a few of which became canonical and still survive. There were many different Targumim, made in different eras to match the current idiom, and in most of them the text was freely translated into a local vernacular and mode of thinking, so that the narrative and poetry took on familiar voice once again. At the same time, in the allegorical and myth-embellished midrash that would later enter the Talmud (as aggadah), the texts were extravagantly interpreted, in all manner of distinctive voices.

Yet translations today often amount to a choice between hearing the text in one voice or none at all. Tradition dictates that one author be imagined, whether the translation is liturgical or scholarly. Too often, in place of an author, there is merely a faceless committee. The Bible's poetry is usually translated as prose, by scholars and clerics unresponsive to the lushly echoing imagery. And when it comes to church and synagogue, the majority of prayers originating in Hebrew, Aramaic, and Greek are translated as indifferently as movie subtitles. The life in those prayers, based largely on psalms and other biblical poetry, is clouded by doctrinaire interpretation.

After ten years' work and additional years of revision, *A Poet's Bible* crystallized for me last year after I had completed the reconstruction and translation of *The Book of J.* I could see how the prose poetry of *J* influenced later poets. The individuality of biblical poetry is the creative jewel of Jewish culture. It appropriated a wide range of Mesopotamian and Canaanite forms, but only recently have a vanguard of scholars traced its assimilation into narrative as well.

We don't know how the Bible looked when it was first written. But we now suspect that most of it was set down as poetic scrolls in widely different eras. *A Poet's Bible* gives a comprehensive view of this original text. Nobody can say what comprises all of the Bible's poetry because the divisions of each book into chapters and verses were the arbitrary choices of editors who lived in later centuries. The scholarly New Oxford Bible refers to the "Writings," more than a third of the Hebrew Bible, as "the poetical books"—and that section of the Bible does not include the books of the prophets nor the *J* portion of the Pentateuch, surely the most poetical text. I have chosen what a scholar can consider a core of poetry in some scrolls—or "books," as we now call them—and translated other books whole.

To speak technically for a moment, the triadic stanza I developed to parallel the original poetry was composed (by extension from the poetics of William Carlos Williams) in handwritten, tristepped lines across the page—that is, with an open possibility of either enjambment or disjunction between the lines and stanzas. I envisioned that a traditional association with the Bible would remain as the lines are centered on the page: the look might suggest a modern liturgy, familiar as an old hymnal.

As I worked, I reread Emily Dickinson, practicing my ear with an American idiom that incorporates an acute sensitivity to the Bible. In particular, Dickinson found a way to defeat and supersede the masculine grandiosity of the King James—as it is read, and not as it is written. What is great about the King James is a sophisticated, plain English that's easily lost in a post-Baroque period. In some ways, Dickinson helped to antiquate its diction and rhyme with her yet more sophisticated and plain American English echoing of it.

The rigorous poetics of Gertrude Stein were also useful to me, as they were for Hemingway and others. In particular, Stein's psychological probings of repetition recalled ancient technique. Besides being a penetrating Old Testament reader like Dickinson, Stein also shared Dickinson's mastery of phrasing and the energetic juxtaposition of high and low diction. Sometimes Stein's ear for poetic prose resembled the *J* writer's, who plays off high diction with low officialese. An obvious example in the *J* text is the representation of Pharaoh's court, in Exodus, as well as in the Joseph cycle of Genesis.

Poets have long been neglected by religious institutions until the most saccharine of verses is mistaken for the genuine article. This insensitivity crosses over to universities. In college textbooks on the Bible as literature, when the authors compare writers of psalms to more recent writers of hymns—to a Martin Luther or an Isaac Watts—they lose all perspective, confusing Luther's religious genius with poetry. No literary critic would count Luther or Watts among the ranks of great poets, but certainly many of the psalmists deserve such respect.

The psalms seem to breathe a different air from modern religious hymns that are born in a parochial setting. The great biblical poems, unlike liturgy, were written by the strongest talents in the mainstream of their high culture. These ancient poets were not writing for a strictly religious audience; most of their work only became liturgy many centuries later. At the time they lived and wrote, the biblical poets were the preeminent writers in their culture, and were not on the poetic periphery.

•   •   •

Both religion and art encourage a step out of time. Once I'd decided to test this relationship by translating the Bible, my childhood religious experience became crucial. My life opened for inspection in a manner I'd only imitated before, influenced by my college instructor, poet Robert Lowell. The effect of my early encounters with two cultures outside the mainstream—the Jewish one and the African-American—came home to me, stronger than any religious practice. Many cultures migrated to America but these two retain their energy. Another, the Puritan culture of New England, nourished Lowell, and although he never said so, I thought of him as coming from an immigrant culture—based upon the older England from which the Puritans sailed.

Bible Music and Soul Music

My parents and grandparents were European immigrants. My maternal grandparents lived out their lives in our home in Detroit, yet stayed within a Yiddish-speaking culture into which I was initiated. By the time I reached first grade at the Yeshiva Beth Yehuda in Detroit, I was dressed in the ageless role of a scholar: tzizes (fringed garment) hanging out of my pants, my soft forelocks resembling the silky beards of my teachers—just as their pale, babylike skin resembled mine. Instead of playground time, we had milk-and-cookies time, and the toothless old men ate and drank along with us.

After my grandfather's death, I found myself in public school among a majority of black students. Aretha Franklin is one Brady classmate I remember: her father was a celebrity, host of Detroit's gospel music hour on the radio; I listened, entranced. Later, I would value African-American culture—its ironic, untamed diction, its music steeped in gospel, the inflections of blues lyrics—aware of how it mirrored my earliest Jewish culture. The senior citizens in both cultures lived close to the youngsters. In black culture, old people danced and jived like the children, so that it made the children seem old beyond their years.

In my kindergarten Yeshiva, the old Jewish men seemed childlike in their femininity: soft, shy, determined, easily moved, withdrawn. We children were taught the same virtues. Most of all we learned to chant, and that is how I remember my first teachers, always chanting. Often from the Bible, of course. And then, I would pass the Christian Pentecostal storefront churches in my neighborhood in the evenings and hear the chantlike surge of song. For some reason it was mostly women who attended—or else they sang the loudest. It was all I knew of any religious culture outside Judaism, but unlike the latter it already was sounding more familiar to me, the foundation for the larger culture of soul music forming in Detroit.

At my bar mitzvah I was a divided boy, baseball pants beneath my suit so I could dash from synagogue to Little League. The test of manhood was managing the division of cultures. Later still, in the contemporary world of art, I would try to engage American culture with a sensibility of an immigrant—pretending or imagining it—since we all once came from the old world, in our various ways.

When I was memorizing Longfellow's "Song of Hiawatha" in the fourth grade, public school represented an anachronistic culture: no grownups I encountered would be caught reading this lengthy mock-epic, much less memorizing it. (Jewish grownups, on the other hand, would study the same Talmud as the kids; black kids might prize the same jazz and soul as the adults.) This irony would not be lost on poet Longfellow, were he still alive—but irony was something I would only learn to appropriate later in life, when Longfellow's High Indian idiom, like T.S. Eliot's High Church idiom, would earn their proper smiles.

• • •

Much of the Hebrew Bible was written by poets who were not parochial writers but more resembled a John Donne or T.S. Eliot: poets first, devotees second. They wrote in the language and imagery of the mainstream culture, whereas now religion finds itself an ancillary culture. Still, the solemn irony of Eliot seemed more distant from the Bible than the flights of soul I loved in Whitman and Dickinson. But the soul poets who truly brought me back to the Bible were the great Hebrew moderns—Bialik, Leah Goldberg, Zelda Mishkovsky, Avot Yeshurun.

First, I had to come back to Hebrew. After the exhilaration of my first translations of psalms, I flew to Israel. While I was there I was invited to appear on a television show, hosted by the poet David Avidan, to read my translations from the Bible.

That night I watched the guests who preceded me on the dressing-room monitor. One was a man who had survived a car-crash coma and described out-of-body experiences when he drove again. The others around me were laughing but I was not yet speaking Hebrew well enough to catch the irony. In fact, I didn't quite catch Avidan's translations of my own psalm translations, as he read them on the air. I tried to smile as I heard some behind-the-camera chuckles. It was nevertheless a revelation to me, this familial merriment about the Bible. Certainly it is sacred, they seemed to be saying, but it is family poetry and we know all its flaws.

Experiences like this helped me to define my own autobiographical voice among the Bible's authors. I'd been educated to think the Bible was half the story of Western cultural origins; classical Greek and Latin was the other half. Yet I found a familiarity with ancient Greek in the Hebrew Bible itself, as I was translating *Ecclesiastes*. This author, known as Qohelet in Hebrew, had absorbed a great deal of Greek literature, and I started to think of him as more modern than I'd expected.

I began to find in the greatest psalms an awareness of the larger world and a cultivated irony in assimilating other literatures. A spirit of inventive dialogue could be discerned throughout early

Hebrew literature, no doubt including many books left out of the biblical canon and now lost. The author of *Ecclesiastes* seemed an especially worldly poet to me, one who put on the mask and speaking voice of King Solomon with a modern tonality in the fourth century B.C. I only follow in his footsteps when I make Solomon's voice my own.

Qohelet, primary author of *Ecclesiastes,* pictured King Solomon as a poet and builder, a renaissance man who embellished his literary career with gardens and vineyards; I modernized this portrayal by giving Solomon a more prominent writing career and returning to him all his attributed books. Solomon's feasts became contemporary parties, his passions my own. I imagined nothing that the original author had not imagined in his own way, but I made the Bible's music more personal—just as Qohelet impersonated the old king in his own image, six centuries later:

> *So I set to work// in the grand style/ building an* oeuvre/ *ten books in five years// works of love and despair/ naked and shameless/ I was married and divorced// I went to all the parties/ the glittering eyes/ and wit: passion-starved// a trail of blinding jewels/ of experience behind me/ more than any king in Jerusalem// I tried on every lifestyle/ I pushed to the center/ through many gaudy affairs// I was surrounded by stars/ singers and dancers/ and fresh young bodies// to choose among/ at the slightest whim/ I was high and I was courted// but I kept my sense of purpose.*

Living English and Doogri

Doogri is the modern Hebrew word for street idiom, and it includes a good many Arabic words as well as some in English. Israeli writers tend to write it about American Jewish academics—"so-and-so knows no doogri"—disparaging a native English speaker whose preferred idiom is a flat one. Doogri is the furnace in which the language remakes itself, and it most resembles slang during the

Elizabethan period, when English was also absorbing many foreign words.

Doogri is a constant reminder that the ancient Hebrew poets, who probably knew several languages, played with current usage by setting it against the echoes of foreign words and officialese. You can sense this more in some books than others: *Job*, for one, plays heavily with Aramaic; *Judith* with Judeo-Greek. To recapture a sense of spokenness in my own work, I needed a judicious use of current idioms and slang, as the original poets did. They were writing for a living audience, not for a colorless, distant future.

My apprenticeship in reclaiming biblical authors began, at nineteen, when I was Robert Lowell's student in New York, Pound in one hand, Rimbaud in the other. Lowell was in the midst of translating from several languages, in a mode he called "imitations." When I began my translations of psalms, ten years later, Lowell was working on Aeschylus' plays; I knew that my command of Hebrew could match his Greek—I admired his ambition and it spurred my own.

One day, another decade later, I was sitting in a barebones Jerusalem café with the Israeli poet, Harold Schimmel. Over glasses of *botz* ("mud" coffee) he was telling me of an earlier visit by Lowell. "He wanted to hear about the Hebrew Bible and how it sounded to us," Schimmel mused. "He was entranced to learn how modern Hebrew poets handled it intimately." As I listened, I could imagine Lowell in Jerusalem, toying with the idea of "imitating" some of the biblical poets, and I knew that imagining the original authors would be a guiding passion for me. Instead of imitation, I thought of my work as "personal" translation—partly to distinguish it from the impersonal surfaces created by committees of translators. Yet I was straining for something further—a dialogue among poets, biblical and contemporary—encouraged by my refurbished ancient surroundings as well as my familiarity with Lowell's heated imagination.

In Israel, where I stayed four years, I learned to think like the contemporary generation of Israeli poets I was editing for a literary magazine. To the Israelis, the American professors who wrote about the Bible's literature were an embarrassment, lacking even Robert Lowell's intuitions about authorship. They simply could not imagine the depths of irony in the Hebrew language. Instead, they wove a blurry web of exegesis around the biblical text. And although the professors paid obsessive attention to that text, the only poetry they found was the skeleton of rhetoric. Perhaps their own imaginative traditions were too heady and uncharted for their abilities: for Jews, it is the tradition of midrash and kabbalah; for Christians, spiritual autobiography.

A Sophisticated Illusion of Oral Tradition

Although I knew that modern writers like Singer or Kafka had Jewish antecedents, it was not until I read the modern Hebrew poets that I imagined the biblical authors as living men and women. Modern translations deliver a false simplicity with smooth clichés, awkward idioms, and undistinguished sound. In almost every case, the simplifiers exchange poetic irony for terse sentiment. But the original biblical irony appears to be an urge for personal encounter (rather than distance), a desire to personalize the written form of poetry and give it a speaking voice. The Hebrew poets gave the Bible a sophisticated quality of spokenness: many of the authors imagined the reader hearing his words rather than reading them, as if the text were not there. This ancient irony echoes the modern literary convention of verisimilitude, lending psychological as well as social reality to fiction and poetry.

So I used my own experience, as the biblical poets had used theirs. I remember the effect of hearing one of my first psalm translations. It was my father's funeral, and at the chapel the rabbi, standing in front of my father's coffin, read it during the eulogy. I had to listen to him read it over the loudspeakers on that literal level, as prayer. Through my pain I heard that he didn't catch my phrasing, and he ignored my lines, echoing the syntax of the King James translation, the music flattened, and the whole, as I'd interpreted it, unraveled. In my old rabbi's defense, I would add that he was born in Europe and American English was not his native tongue.

Now, I imagine prayer as idealized speaking, out into the realm of eternal time. It requires a literary trade-off for poets: you don't write letters home to your parents in verse, yet in this instance—verse as prayer—you speak as if to a spiritual parent. If the literary practitioners at King Solomon's court included even one great poet (and I presume there were several) it would be no surprise that he or she was revered because he or she would not compromise her art for rigid devotion. Even now we're assured by Freud, in *Totem and Taboo*, that "in only a single field of our civilization has the omnipotence of thoughts been retained, and that is in the field of art."

Yet art has its early and late periods of renaissance in religious culture too, where the writer remains sovereign. Gershom Scholem described the medieval Kabbalah as achieving "an astounding loosening of the concept of Revelation. Here the authority of Revelation also constitutes the basis of the freedom in its application and interpretation." That is to say, religion could—in the hands of a few masters of the Kabbalah—become the vehicle for a liberating art.

The Hebraic poets of the Bible also felt confident enough to reinterpret their culture, breaking free of conventional pieties. If we can imagine that these poets gave more life to the character of God than we've yet come to know, we regain an ability to see ourselves.

The Body's Call

PSALMS

SONG OF SOLOMON

LAMENTATIONS

MACCABEES

JOB

ECCLESIASTES

Psalms

ONE DAY, translating a psalm that I thought was written in anger
and is usually presented as such, I suddenly realized it was not
anger at all but an intense depression, a self-conscious awareness
of failure. The psalmist was facing depression and not allowing
himself to respond with anger. Instead, even as his voice speaks
bitterly, he overcomes despair with his song's ironic sense of never
ending, echoing into eternity. And I felt the poet's utterly real
presence.

Psalms was written by as many as a hundred poets over seven
centuries. Judaic culture went through great changes in that span,
and consequently the Lord appealed to in one psalm may seem a
different deity from the Lord in another. A unity is nonetheless
maintained in the personal bonding with that Lord, and this rela-
tionship is clearest in the ancient Hebrew, where God's original
names were used. Normally we think of relations with a lord or
king as highly formal, but the psalmists bring us into the intimate
realm of his kingdom.

I was provoked to reencounter the Bible by the psalm transla-
tions of Philip Sidney and his sister, the Countess of Pembroke,
in Elizabethan England. I hadn't imagined the original poems to
be as sophisticated in idiom as their translations suggested, but
now they seem more accurate than the King James translation,
where the wordplay is weak. Although Sidney and Pembroke
worked from Latin, they adapted all manner of Italianate forms—
they were playing with their own language, a relatively new lan-
guage then, as Hebrew was for the psalmists.

What better analogy for the court of King David than Queen

Elizabeth's, who was not only a patron of poets but known to have written verse herself. As the lyrics of Renaissance Europe were often free variations on the classical Latin originals, many of the psalms seemed to me spirited caricatures of early Hebrew and Canaanite cult liturgies.

Although formally intricate, a speaking voice penetrates the texture of many psalms, often punning on officious religious phrases. The resemblance to a modern poem is striking, since the texture of phrasing can unify a free-verse poem in a similar manner. And the psychological situation of a poet struggling to hear himself—to let his voice counterpoint the poem's texture—parallels a psalmist's simulated dialogue with his or her God. The appeal to a higher order or music lifts the poem in each instance out of monologue.

In early translations by English poets, the tones of classical convention—of invoking the muses—amplify the Hebrew convention of speaking to the deity. At its origins, however, the biblical psalm exhibits an even greater range of speaking tones. Yet today, poetry mostly sheds the ghosts of the muses. Without standard criterions of diction, a poem is almost an act of faith itself as it gropes toward discovering its own inclusive form. As a poet, in that act of discovery I'm both speaking and listening to myself speak. And in that way I draw closer to the psalmist's enactment of voice.

The drive toward realism in the psalmists is remarkable. A series of seemingly unrelated images in a given psalm creates not a tapestry, but a psychological atmosphere of reality. It's a self-conscious realism, and I imagine it as music, and in particular the blues, whose sobering irony often developed from spiritual hymns. Some of the early psalmists appear to be musicians as well, their texts serving as lyrics; many of their names indicate musical collaboration, Korah and Asaph the most prevalent. Other psalmists seem to me fundamentally writing poets. Of the twenty-one psalms I've chosen, each sounds to me as if written by a different poet.

❦ *Psalms* ❧

PSALM 1

Happy the one
stepping lightly over
paper hearts of men

and out of the way
of mind-locked reality
the masks of sincerity

he steps from his place at the glib café
to find himself in the word
of the infinite

embracing it
in his mind
with his heart

parting his lips for it
lightly
day into night

transported like a tree
to a riverbank
sweet with fruit in time

his heart unselfish
whatever he does
ripens

while bitter men turn dry
blowing in the wind
like yesterday's paper

unable to stand
in the gathering
light

they fall
faded masks
in love's spotlight

burning hearts of paper
unhappily
locked in their own glare

but My Lord opens
his loving one
to breathe embracing air.

P S A L M 6

Lord, I'm just a worm
don't point to me
in frozen anger

don't let me feel
I more than deserve
all your rage

but mercy, Lord, let me feel mercy
I'm weak, my spirit so dark
even my bones shiver

my shadow surrounds me—I'm shocked
how long, Lord, how long
till you return to shine your light

return to me dear Lord
bring back the light
that I can know you by

because those that are dead
have no thought of you
to make a song by

I'm tired of my groaning
my bed is flowing away
in the nights of tears

depression like a moth
eats from behind my face,
tiny motors of pain push me

get out of here all you
glad to see me so down
your every breath so greased with vanity

My Lord is listening so high
my heavy burden of life floats up
as a song to him

let all my enemies shiver
on the stage of their total self-consciousness
and all their careers ruined in one night.

PSALM 8

My Lord Most High
your name shines
on the page of the world

from behind the lights
covering the heavens—
my lips like infants

held to the breast
grow
to stun the darkest thoughts

when I look up
from the work of my fingers
I see the moon and stars

your hand set there
and I can barely think
what is a man

how did you spare a thought for him
care to remember
his line

descending through death
yet you let him rise
above himself, toward you

held by music of words . . .
you set his mind in power
to follow the work of your hand

laying the world at his feet
all that is nameable
all that changes through time

from canyons to the stars
to starfish
at bottom of the sea

all that moves blazing a path
in air or water
or deep space of imagination on paper

My Lord Most High
your name shines
on the page of the world.

P S A L M   1 2

Help, My Lord
where's the man
who loves you

where's the child
with human truth
behind him

helping him walk—
he grows into a lie
with his neighbors around him

speaking from made-up hearts
he becomes an empty letter
his lips sealed

tongue dried up
in its coat of vanity
its web of pride

"our lips belong to us
do what we want
to rise in the world

we don't want to hear
anything higher"
"I'm called I appear

by the human voice
the conscious victim
I send words to lift

whoever's waiting
I release him from lips
swollen in authority"

these words are free
like released energy
without violence

finite matter
broken open
with the tenderness of dawn

these words were always yours
My Lord, you sent into the present
lifting us from the inhuman

you are behind us
with every step in the infinite
through the swollen crowd around us

living lies
in a chain of lips
holding their children.

PSALM 19

The universe unfolds
the vision within:
creation

stars and galaxies
the words and lines
inspired with a hand

day comes to us
with color and shape
and night listens

and what is heard
breaks through deep silence
of infinite space

the rays come to us
like words
come to everyone

human on earth
we are the subjects
of light

a community
as it hears
the right words

creating time
the space of the sky
the face of the nearest star

that beats like a heart
in the tent where it sleeps
near the earth every night

then rises above the horizon
growing in our awareness
of the embrace

of inspiration
we feel as we turn
toward the warmth

starting at the edge of the sky
to come over us
like a secret love we wait for

love we can't hide
our deepest self-image
from

nobody holds back that fire
or closes the door
of time

words My Lord writes shine
opening me
to witness myself

conscious and unconscious
complex mind
warmed in an inner lightness

that moves me
to the simple beat
of time

testimony
of one author
speaking through history's pages

commanding my attention
bathed in light
around me

clean perfect notes
hearts play
make us conscious

we become the audience
amazed we can feel
justice come over us

our minds become real
unfold
the universe within

silence becomes real
we hear
clear words

become the phrasing of senses
lines of thought
stanzas of feeling

more lovely than gold
all the gold in the world
melting to nothing in light

sweet flowing honey
the right words
in my mouth

warming your subject
as he listens
breaking through his reflection

his image in the mirror
what mind can understand the failure
waiting in itself

silent self-image
created in the dark alone
to hold

power over others!
but justice comes over us
like a feeling for words that are right

absolutely
a mirror is pushed away
like a necessary door

we're free to look at everything
every shape and color
light as words

opening the mind
from nightmares of social failure
desperate routines

we're inspired above
the surface parade
of men dressed up in power

we see the clear possibility
of life growing
to witness itself

let these words
of my mouth
be sound

the creations
of my heart
be light

so I can see myself
free of desperate symbols
mind-woven coverings

speechless fears
images hidden within
we are the subjects of light

opening to join you
vision itself
my constant creator.

P S A L M 2 2

Lord, My Lord, you disappear
so far away
unpierced by my cry

my sigh of words
all day My Lord
unheard

murmur of groans at night
then silence
no response

while you rest
content
in the songs of Israel

in the trust of fathers
you delivered
who cried to you

they were brought home
warm and alive
and inspired

but I am a worm
sub-human
what men come to

with a hate of their own futures
despised
and cheered like a drunk

staggering across the street
they howl after him
like sick dogs

"Let the Lord he cried to
save him
since they were so in love"

you brought me through the womb
to the sweetness
at my mother's breasts

no sooner my child eyes
looked around
I was in your lap

you are My Lord
from the time my mother found
me inside

make yourself appear
I am surrounded
and no one near

a mad crowd
tightens a noose around me
the ring of warheads

pressing ravenous noses
the mad whispering of
gray technicians

the water of my life evaporates
my bones stick through the surface
my heart burns down like wax

melting into my stomach
my mouth dry as a clay cup
dug up in the yard

I've fallen into the mud
foaming dogs surround me
ghost men

pierce my hands and feet
my bones stare at me
in disbelief

men take my clothes
like judges
in selfish dreams

make yourself appear
My Lord show me
the power

to free my life from chains
of bitter command
from the mouths of ghost men

trained on my heart
like a city
save me from mindless

megaphones of hate
you've always heard me
from my human heart

allowed me to speak
in the air of your name
to men and women

all who know fear
of losing yourselves
in vacant cities

speak to him
Israel's children
sing with him

all seed of men
show your faces
amazed in love

he does not despise them
he has not disappeared
from the faces of earth

from the ground of the worm
or the ear of the victim
I will always repeat

this song of life
with my hand that is free
from men who need victims

may our hearts live forever!
and the furthest reaches of space
remember our conscious moment

inspiring light
like those disappeared from memory
returned to the planet's earth

everyone has to appear
at death's door
everyone falls to the ground

while his seed carries on
writing and speaking
to people still to come

who remember to sing
how generous My Lord appears
to those hearing.

P S A L M   2 3

The Lord is my shepherd
and keeps me from wanting
what I can't have

lush green grass is set
around me and crystal water
to graze by

there I revive with my soul
find the way that love makes
for his name   and though I pass

through cities of pain, through death's living shadow
I'm not afraid to touch
to know what I am

your shepherd's staff is always there
to keep me calm
in my body

you set a table before me
in the presence of my enemies
you give me grace to speak

to quiet them
to be full with humanness
to be warm in my soul's lightness

to feel contact every day
in my hand and in my belly
love coming down to me

in the air of your name, Lord
in your house
in my life.

PSALM 30

High praises
to you who raised me
up

so my critics fall silent
from their death wishes
over me

Lord Most High
I called you
and I was made new

you pulled me back
from the cold lip of the grave
and I am alive

to sing to you
friends, play in his honor
band of steady hearts

his anger like death
passes in a moment
his love lasts forever

cry yourself to sleep
but when you awake
light is all around you

I thought I was experienced
nothing was going to shake me
I was serious as a mountain

Lord, you were with me and then
you were gone
I looked for your face in terror

my body was made of clay
My Lord, it is now
I call you

what good is my blood my tears
sinking in the mud
is mere dust singing

can it speak
these words on my tongue, Lord
help me

turn my heavy sighing into dance
loosen my shirt and pants
and wrap me in your glow

so my heart can find its voice
through my lips to you
warm and alive

rising
above all bitterness
high praises.

PSALM 36

Inside my heart I hear
how arrogance talks
to himself without fear

hidden from eyes
he flatters himself
but we see him on the faces

of false faces and words
thinking—even asleep—
how to squeeze love out

from feelings from words
how to put wisdom on her back
then hold his miniature knowledge back

your love fills a man, Lord
with a kind of air
making him lighter

he rises in measure of your judgment
above the mountains of thought
above the clouds of feeling

the strength of his measure stays
in the eyes returning to mountains
from the surface of the sea

he falls like any animal
standing up only by your mercy
his children grow in the shadow of your wings

feast on gourmet fare in your house
with water that sparkles from wells
beyond the reach of a mind

the fountain of life
is lit
by your light

you extend your embrace
to those who feel you are there
keep holding the loving

keep us from being crushed
by arrogant feet
by the hand of pride

the powerful are falling over themselves
their minds have pulled them down
there they will lie, flung down.

PSALM 49

Now hear this, world
all who live in air
important, ordinary, poor

my lips are moved by a saying
my heart whispers
in sound sense

I measure with my ear
this dark message and it opens
around my lyre

why should I make fear
dog my steps
growl in my thoughts

when the masters of vanity
breed in public for attention
rolling in scraps of money

no man can build a way
to God outside his body
to buy his continual release

to pay a ransom in every moment
for the gift of living
the price higher than his power to think

so that he could live forever
blind to his own falling
into the pit of death

but we all can see
the wisest man dies
along with the cunningly petty

their fortunes pass like mumbled words
among others
above their graves

it is there in hardened silence
the inheritors will join them
their bodily measure of earth

and though they put their names
on spaces of land,
their inward thoughts like words,

the mouths wither around them—
prosperous men
lose their intelligence

remember that in its saying
like animals who leave nothing to quote
those men pass on totally self-centered

like sheep gathered into the earth
their followers headlong after them
death's herd

their flesh stripped in death's store
and the big show made standing upright
erased in the sunrise

but My Lord holds the ransom
for death's vain embrace
as this music holds me—inside

don't be afraid of the big man
who builds a house that seems to grow
to the pride of his family

nothing will lie between
his body with its pride
and the ground he falls to

the life he made happy for himself
"so men may praise you
in your prosperity"

will find the company
of his fathers
around him as total darkness

his inward thoughts like words
the mouth withers around—
prosperous men lose their intelligence.

PSALM 58

Can this be justice
this pen to hold
they that move my arm

to follow them—blind stars?
They think I have submitted
to the vicious decorum of fame?

Oh generation come from dust
Oh no: you steel yourselves
to write; your hands

weigh, like a primitive scale,
selfish desire unfulfilled . . .
strangers from the womb

no sooner born and here
than chasing after
impulsive wishes

for which they will lie, cheat, kill.
Cancerous cold desire
gnaws in their brain

as the doctor
the greatest virtuoso specialist
numbs their consciousness

cutting into the chest
exposing the vital organ
totally blind to the truth.

Lord, cramp their fingers
till the arms hang limp like sausage,
grind down to sand

the teeth of the power-hungry
and let their selves dissolve into it
like ebbing tide on a junk-strewn beach

and when they in profound bitterness
unsheathe the sharpened thought
cut it out of their brain, Love!

make them disappear like snails
slime of their bodies melting away
or like babies, cord cut in abortion

to be thrown out as discharge
eyes withered in the daylight
though they never looked at it.

And let the children of greed like weeds
be pulled from their homes
and their parents blown away like milkweed . . .

The loving man will be revived
by this revenge and step ashore
from the bloodlust of the self-righteous

so that every man can say
there is justice so deep
a loving man has cause to sing.

PSALM 7 3

My Lord is open
to Israel, to all hearts
within hearing

but I turned and
almost fell   moved
by flattery spoken

through transparent shrouds
impressing me
with the power of imagery

and fame of the mind
loving to strut
in its mirror

with its unfelt body
smooth as a machine
without a care in the world

prosperous mouthpieces
in their material cars
of pride

and suits of status
covering up
crookedness

their eyes
are walls
for wish-images

their mouths big
cynical
megaphones

self-made gods
whose words envelop the heads of men
hiding their fears

they go through the world
in self-encasing roles
in which they will die

lowered in heavy caskets
they made themselves
out of words

but meanwhile they suck in
most people
draining their innocence

until everyone believes
God isn't there
no wonder these men prosper

they push through the world
their violence
makes them secure

it seemed I opened my heart
and hand
stupidly

every day had its torture
every morning
my nerves were exposed

I was tempted to hide
to kill the moment
with pride

instead I tried to know you
and keep your song alive
but my mind was useless

until my heart opened
the cosmic door
to a continual presence

that is you
lighting the future
above the highway

down which self-flattering men
travel in style
to prisons of mind-locked time

they have their pleasures
cruelly pursued
and you urge them

to their final reward
you let them rise on dead bodies
so they have to fall

like a bad dream
the moment you awake
they are gone forever

my mind was dry thought
my feelings drained
through dusty clay

I was blindly
eating through life
like a moth in wool

I was crude
too proud
to know you

yet continually with you
take my hand
in love

it sings with you
inspired advice
leading to your presence

what will I want
but continual inspiration
in the present with you

what else will I find
in the blues of the sky
but you

and me in you
where am I in what universe
without you

my body dies of exhaustion
but you are the mountain
lifting my open heart

higher than a mind can go
into the forever
into the future

men who hide in their hearts
have bitter minds
they will lose

those people become no one
leaving you for an ideology
for a material car

but I waited for you
I was open, My Lord
to find my song

I found you here
in music I continue
to hear

with each new breath
expanding
to give me space.

PSALM 82

My Lord is the judge
at the heart
in the infinite

speaking through time and space
to all gods
he let be

"instead of lips
smoothed by success
and appearances

defend your silent critic
locked in barred categories
his conscience

painfully opened
by vicious systems
release him

let him speak
break the grip
of the prosperous

whose things enclose them
from the lightness of knowledge
the openness of understanding

they build in darkness
burying justice
digging at the foundation

of earth and men
the orbit
of trust"

I was thinking
you too are gods
heads of nations

thoughts of My Lord
but you will disappear
like the spirit you silence

your heads fall
like great nations
in ruins

My Lord, open
their consciousness
to share your judgment

all nations are men
you hear
beyond categories.

PSALM 90

Lord, you are our home
in all time
from before the mountains rose

or even the sun
from before the universe
to after the universe

you are Lord forever
and we are home
in your flowing

you turn men into dust
and you ask them to return
children of men

for a thousand years
in your eyes
are a single day

yesterday
already passed
into today

a ship in the night
while we were present
in a human dream

submerged
in the flood of sleep
appearing in the morning

like new grass
growing into afternoon
cut down by evening

we are swept off our feet
in an unconscious wind
of war or nature

or eaten away
with anxiety
worried to death

worn-out swimmers
all dressed up
in the social whirl

you see our little disasters
secret lusts
broken open in the light

of your eyes
in the openness
penetrating our lives

every day melts away
before you
our years run away

into a sigh
at the end
of a story

over in another breath
seventy years
eighty—gone in a flash

and what was it?
a tinderbox of vanity
a show of pride

and we fly apart
in the empty mirror
in the spaces between stars

in the total explosion of galaxies
how can we know ourselves
in this human universe

without expanding
to the wonder that you are
infinite lightness

piercing my body
this door of fear
to open my heart

our minds are little stars
brief flares
darkness strips naked

move us to see your present
as we're moved to name each star
lighten our hearts with wonder

return
and forgive us
locking our unconscious

behind the door
and as if it isn't there
as if we forget we're there

we walk into space unawed
unknown to ourselves
years lost in thought

a thousand blind moments
teach us when morning comes
to be moved

to see ourselves rise
returning witnesses
from the deep unconscious

and for every day lost
we find a new day
revealing where we are

in the future and in the past
together again
this moment with you

made human for us
to see your work
in the open-eyed grace of children

the whole vision unlocked
from darkness
to the thrill of light

where our hands reach for another's
opening to life
in our heart's flow

the work of this hand
flowing open
to you and from you.

PSALM 101

The city of your love
sings through me
before you, My Lord

you hold my writing hand
that makes my living
creative act

won't you come to me?
I sit here in my house
with an open heart

no willful image
blocks the door,
I just won't see

the theatrics of personality
crowding
the openness you allow

this art that hurts
those with ears for only jewelry
they go far away

locked within themselves
their self-flattery
I've reduced to silence

their narrow eyes
inflated pride
blown away

I'm always looking
for your people
to share this space

the contact of imagination
inspired
by necessity

beyond the stage doors
of weak characters
cut off from real streets

no more precious actors
costumed in sound
to litter this town with clichés

every morning
I silence with your light
desperate images

they run away
from the city of your name
that calls an open heart.

PSALM 114

When Israel came out of Egypt
like a child suddenly free
from a people of strange speech

Judah became a home
for the children of Israel
as they became a sanctuary

for the God of their fathers:
Once, this House of Israel
stammered into the open

and as the sea saw them coming
it ran from the sight
the Jordan stopped dead in its tracks

mountains leaped like frightened rams
hills were a scattering flock
of lambs

What was so alarming, sea?
Jordan, what vision
drained your strength away?

Mountains, why did you quake
like fearful rams?
Hills, why did you jump like lambs?

Earth, tremble again, again
in the presence
of your maker's voice

it was the God of Jacob
and he is here
all around you

a sudden pool of water
from a desert rock
a fountain from wilderness stone—

life from a heart of stone
and from bitter tears
sweet-spoken land.

PSALM 121

I look up and find a mountain
to know inside
then light appears

inspired from most high
My Lord, creator
of earth and sky

we shall not be moved
this power inside
never fell asleep

over Israel
My Lord is in the light
the atmosphere

the power that moves my hand
through the sunlight that doesn't melt me
and by the moonlight

that moves us inside
to be inspired
above burning pride

desire
which is the mountain of our life
held in his air

and by his hand
we're free
to be moved

we may come and go
from now
to forever.

PSALM 1 3 0

I am drowning
deep in myself, Lord
I'm crying

I'm calling you
hear this voice, Lord
find me in your ears

the mercy of your attention
as it looks through the shell
of my selfishness

if you see only
vain impulses
marking the body's surface

the lines in the face
then there is no one
who'd hold up his head

but you allow us forgiveness
allow a song
coming through us

to you
as I call to you
as I rely on these words

as I wait
for you
more certain than dawn

through the steady ticking till morning
wait, Israel
even when watches seem to stop

My Lord comes to me
in a rush of love
setting my heart free

into a bright sky
we are lightened
in the mercy of his attention.

PSALM 133

It's so good, the turn of a season
people living for a moment as equals
secure in the human family

as sweet as spring rain
making the beard silky
Aaron's beard

his robes sparkle
rich with heaven's simple jewels
like the crown of dew

on Lebanon's Mt. Hermon
shared equally on the hills
of Israel

where the Lord graces our eyes
fresh from reborn wonder
as if we'd live forever.

PSALM 137

Into the rivers of Babylon
we cried like babies, loud
unwilling to move

beyond the memory
the flowing blood
of you, Israel

to an orchestra of trees
we lent our harps
silently leaning

when the enemy shoved us
"asking" tender songs of Israel
under heavy chains

"give us songs of Israel!"
as if we could give our mouths
to a strange landlord . . .

If I forget thee
sweet Jerusalem
let my writing hand wither

my tongue freeze to ice
sealing up my voice
my mind numb as rock

if I forget
your kiss
Jerusalem on my lips . . .

My Lord
remembers you, Edomites
Jerusalem raped vivid as daylight

you who screamed to strip her
strip her naked
to the ground

Oh Lady Babylon
Babylon the destroyer
lucky man who holds you

who crushes you
who opens your mind
to wither instantly in air

who holds up your crying babies
as if to stun them
against solid rock.

PSALM 139

There's nothing in me, My Lord
that doesn't open to your eyes
you know me when I sit

you note when I arise
in the darkest closet of my thought
there is an open window of sunshine for you

you walk with me
lie down with me
at every move await me

at every pause
you know the words
my tongue will print in air

if I say yes
you have already nodded
no—and you have shaken your head

in any doubts I lose my way
I find your hand
on me

such knowledge so high
I can never reach with a mind
or hold any longer than a breath

to get away from you
I could let my imagination fly
but you would hold it in your sky

or I could sleep with the dead in the ground
but your fire from the depths
would awaken me

I could fly on gold ray of sun
from dawn in east
west to stars of night

and your hand
would point the way
and your right hand hold me steady

however close I pull the night around me
even at midnight
day strips me naked

in your tender sight
black and white
are one—all light

you who put me together
piece by piece in the womb
from light

that work shines
through the form of my skeleton
on my song of words

you watched as my back steadied
the still-soft fuselage of ribs
in primitive studio deep within

you saw me as putty
a life unfashioned
a plane at the bottom of the sea

and the great book of its life
this embryo will write
in a body you have sculpted

My Lord—your thoughts
high and precious
beyond logic like stars

or like grains of sand I try to count
I fall asleep and awake
on the beach of your making

My Lord—stop the breath
of men who live by blood
alone and lie to your face

who think they can hide
behind the same petty smile
they use to smear your name

My Lord—you hear me hate
back your haters
with total energy

concentrated
in one body
that is yours and mine

My Lord—look at me
to see my heart
test me—to find my mind

if any bitterness lives here
lead me out
into the selfless open.

Song of Solomon

THE ARAMAIC *targumim* (ancient translations) of the *Song of Solomon* are allegorical, taking the kind of liberties with the Hebrew that we would call fiction. The text is easily allegorized because it already embodies a transformation of imagery in King Solomon's original composition. Some of the imagery comes from ancient Canaanite ritual songs for mythological marriage rites. By transforming a pagan liturgy into a poem of passion, human and divine, Solomon demythologized it.

It's fashionable among some biblical scholars to read the *Song of Songs* (as the poem is also known) as if it were a collection of secular love songs. This turns the poem into another allegory, a modern one of sensuality. But the imagery in the original text reflects a powerful and characteristic type of early Jewish irony, a provocative appropriation of pagan liturgical style in which the lovers were gods, and the occasion of anxiety, fertility rites. The imagery, as transmuted in the *Song of Solomon,* comes free of its ritual usage; the emotional anxiety of the lover is personally felt.

I find the poem to be sophisticated, the narrator assuming the dream persona of his lover as well as the voices of a chorus (in order to satirize those ancient conventions, as Greek poets often did). I've translated the fifth chapter of the *Song of Solomon,* although I don't believe the original was divided into chapters. In fact, I would suggest that we have only a fragment of the original poem, much of it edited by later, priestly hands.

The editors did not forget that the great king was the author. It makes sense that Solomon was a serious poet, given the reputation of his father, David. And unlike his father, he had the benefit of a court education. He no doubt encouraged a large retinue of poets at his own court, of which more than one might have collaborated with him on the *Song of Solomon*. These professional poets would also have found exotic sources for the poem in Canaanite forms, knowing Solomon's reputation as lover to many wives of non-Jewish origin.

In this portion of the poem, the female protagonist's anxiety about Solomon suggests the poet was familiar with longing. Perhaps at the time he was deeply in love with a new wife. And yet I can also imagine him as a father, consoling a lovesick daughter. I suspect the poet received much support (if not direct help) from the woman in question. She would have appreciated the way the king personalized the customs of mythical and earthly love, and how he localized the scene in Jerusalem.

SONG OF SOLOMON

I will be in my garden
as I am deep within you
my bride

as if you are my sister
I am rich in spices—
as if my bride, I pluck fresh myrrh

I am rich with honey
and I will eat the honeycomb whole
as well

I will have my wine, my bride
and it is pure, my sister
as milk and honey

friend, you will eat
you will drink deeply, lover
you will be rich with love, my dearest friend

I was asleep
but the soul within me
stayed awake

like my heart—true to a timeless rhythm
to which I still respond—
listen, a gentle knocking

like my heart's beating—
Open to me, my love
my purest image, sister, dove

all I can imagine—my head is drenched
with dew, all my memories
melt into you

I would walk through nights of blinding rain
all doors locked to my presence
I would be happy in blackest exile

knowing you alone would not reject me
never forget
not turn away—

. . .

But I've undone the robe of devotion
where I wrapped my naked heart before you—
how can I rise to your presence?

I've washed the feet that were tired and dirty
when I walked in the reality of your presence—
how can I stand and face myself?

. . .

My love who came inside me
whom I held firmly
whose hand was on the lock of my being

removed his arms
pulled his hand away—
I awoke and

I was drawn to him
a softness spread in me
I was open within

and then I was desolate and empty
he had gone
my heart leapt from my breast

I ran to the door
my soul overwhelmed me
my hands were drenched, as if with perfume

it was my love for him—
the lock was wet with the myrrh
of my devotion

I opened for my love
I alone was open to him
but he had gone

the one for whom I trembled
heard it from my lips
how I had turned from him when

I thought I was alone—
suddenly my soul no longer knew me
just as I had forgotten him

I was riveted with anxiety
I was as lifeless as an empty robe
I couldn't move

my feet were a statue's feet
I was lifeless clay
I was naked earth

then I wandered through the streets
looking for signs of his nearness
seeing nothing

I called, I cried
desperate for his closeness
hearing only silence

only my enemies heard me, like watchmen
patrolling my city's walls
who found me in night gown

who saw me vulnerable and alone
who struck me down
I was wounded for my distraction

my robe my dignity stripped away
I could not even pray
my heart was in my mouth

but now, nations of the world, I warn you
when you see my love
when you turn toward Jerusalem

you will say I bore all for him
the pain and loss was love for him
I was his to the core

"But what makes your love any better than ours
what makes you so beautiful
that he leaves you, and you search for him?

How is your love better than any other
that you stoop from your ivory tower
daring to warn us?"

My love is white with radiance
red with vigorous strength
unmistakable—a banner leading the way

over the heads of a great army
and his head more inspiring than a crown of gold
his hair a raven-black flame

a dove's eyes, clear
beside a soothing river
reflecting its depth, brimming

pools of tenderness—
indestructible jewels
set in whites of kindness

his gaze a penetrating shaft of light
so deft
it is milk—warm and familiar

his words are riverbanks, firm
lush spice beds
a lingering perfume

to remind you of his lips
which are roses
his beard a soft bed of grass

to lean against like a page of his words
bathed in transparent dew
flowing with myrrh

his arms form a vessel of gold
to hold me secure
as a voyager to Tarshish

his will is a sail
and his desires
are a steady wind

his belly is polished ivory—
and strong, clear as azure
is his skin—a cloudless sky

his legs are firm columns
fine as marble
and his feet like golden pedestals—

columns of a scroll, words of spun gold—
his appearance naturally noble as
Lebanon cedars swaying in the breeze

his breath a delicious breeze
words a golden nectar
sustenance and delight

he is altogether delightful—
this is my love
and this my true friend

who never abandons me
a love so pure
you will know it unmistakably

when you turn toward Jerusalem
nations of the world
and all your sons and daughters.

(Chapter 5)

Lamentations

THERE ARE several laments that comprise *Lamentations,* each by a different poet. No doubt there were dozens of similar laments and elegies by poets who were not included but who helped create the Hebrew elegiac tradition.

The poet who composed the third and most personal chapter of *Lamentations* probably wrote psalms and prophetic poetry as well, since this poem radiates formal mastery. The daughter of Zion whose voice laments throughout the book seems a particularly vulnerable sensibility in this poem, and at this early date I found it only realistic to imagine the author as a woman. At the time of writing, her poem was passed from hand to hand, her seal a mark of genius. Not yet a chapter in a book, this poem may have been collected by the circle of poets returning to Jerusalem from exile in Babylon.

The lament was already an ancient form when this great Hebrew poet lived, and it was central to the ancestral tradition of women prophets. Long before, Sumerian laments over the destruction of cities were being composed as Abram left Ur for Canaan; usually these compositions were put into the mouth of the ruined city's goddess. The Jewish poet of *Lamentations* assimilated this form to a Judaic vision. She transformed the patron goddess of ancient cities into the daughter of Zion, who is no goddess but only a metaphor to convey feelings of loss—the loss of people, first, and then homeland.

The voice in *Lamentations* faces a God who allows his one Temple to be destroyed. The poets make his loss intensely personal, probably within a generation of the actual event, in 587 B.C.

There is no justifying the catastrophe, and no easy comfort in absolute answers. As Jerusalem personified, the poet does not turn suffering into a condition for redemption. We are losers, she admits, yet we share the disaster with the deity. In worldly terms, the poet remains alive to the reality of an imperfect world, and that worldview was probably assimilated in Babylon along with the complex acrostic form of the poem.

This Jewish poet founds her work on typically Hebraic calls to prophecy: the need to bear witness and to dramatize vulnerability. The unspeakable is given a peculiarly Jewish voice that confronts the mysteries, silences, and abandonments of the ancient religions of that time with personal testimony. No event could be too sacred for Jewish poets, who now found themselves writing in exile in Babylon.

Although born into the literate upper class, the poet might have been a widow or orphan of a Levite (a class of liturgical scribes and musicians) and any religious prohibitions against her authorship would have been broken in the devastation of exile. Centuries later, tradition would ascribe her poem to the prophet Jeremiah, but I've tried to restore the original author's poem in its idiomatic yet strict stanzas. Formally complex, the poem manages to contrast the daughter of Zion's intimate speech with a choric response—a vestigial chorus—in its refrain.

❧ Lamentations ❧

ALEPH

It is I who have seen
with just human eyes

suffering beyond the power of men
to know is there

a wrath so deep
we are struck dumb

and we are sheep
seized by animal terror

defenseless before a world unleashed
from anything human

we have seen its frenzy raised like an arm
but we feel our shepherd's blow

BET

He has led me into darkness
a valley no light can reach

nothing to illumine the smallest step I take
though I follow what he alone may teach

he has turned against me
with the arm that pointed my way

it is I alone who felt his hand
all sleepless night and day again

he reduced me to skin and bones
my skin was paper for his heavy hand

I was under siege
I was herded into ghettoes

GHIMEL

My mind was utterly stranded
surrounded by seas of poverty

he let me sit in the dark
until I could not think

I was sealed up in a tomb
with the ancient dead

I was fenced in like sheep
I was locked in an empty room

I was bound in chains
I could not turn around

I could not stand up to pray
he had turned away

DALET

I would cry after him for help
my throat was dry as clay

all my hopes came to roadblocks
all my dreams to barbed wire

inside myself I was exposed in a desert
all my ways arrived at despair

he was a scorpion in my path
a lion crouching in the brush

he had become my nightmare
a mad bear in my tracks

a cancer waiting inside me
a fear of being torn to pieces

HEY

He had mauled my confidence
I was a living horror

all the world turned its eyes away
I crawled in the desert

I was his target
I was pinned in the center of his sight

I was pierced in my vital organs
I had lost control of my bowels

I was a laughingstock to the world
he made me their cruelest joke

he passed me the cup of bitterness
he made me drunk with tears

VAV

I was dazed with wormwood
I was in a deadly stupor

he pressed my face in the dust
I had ground my teeth to bits

I have woken with my heart in pieces
I have breakfasted on ashes

my life was pulled from my grasp
my soul was in exile

I was a hollow shell
I was a stranger to myself

peace was a dry husk, an empty word
I was blown in the wind

6 3

Lamentations

Z A Y E N

I forgot what goodness means
shalom meant nothing to me

and I thought: my spirit is dead
hope in God is beyond me

I was broken down, mumbling
I was shattered by anxiety

the more I thought about my suffering—
remembering the agony of my losses—

the more I tasted wormwood
turning to poison within me

and now, still, I remember everything
my soul staggers into exile:

H E T

Memory the weight on my back
and deep in my breast every crushing detail

I cannot close my eyes before it
I cannot rise from my bed

and yet I do each day
and I rouse my heart

that the memory itself so vividly lives
awakens a deathless hope

loving-kindness like air
cannot be used up

though I breathe heavily, locked in a room
beyond the wall a wind blows freely

T E T

The Lord's mercy brings a new morning
each day awakens the thought of him

though I'm buried in nights of doubt
day returns faithfully—he's always there

"The Lord is all that I have"
calls my soul and my heart responds

my hope lives within, infinite as mercy
how else could I *remember* it!

the Lord is good to me
because I do not turn and run

his goodness does not disappear
to the heart turning to him:

Y O D

Remembering in the turning
trusting in the memory

how good to find patience
to let rejected hope return

and how good to learn
to bear the burden young

to sit silent and alone
when the weight falls on your shoulders

to feel the weight of your maker
as all hope seems lost

to put your mouth to dust
(perhaps living is still worthwhile)

•   •   •

To turn your cheek to its striker
to be overwhelmed by abuse

to face the worst
to drink your fill of disgrace

to swallow mockery of things held dear
to survive the poison of humiliation

•   •   •

K A P H

How good to be desolate and alone
because the Lord does not reject forever

after the intensity of anger
mercy returns in a firm embrace

because his love lasts forever
beyond anything we can know

no matter how far away
he does not abandon his creation

we were not tormented lightly
yet nothing in him desired suffering

he didn't desire to make us earth's prisoners
returning to the dust at our feet

L A M E D

And when men lower us in their eyes
cheapen our right to be ourselves

when we are brutalized by "universal" justice
subverting the word "justice" itself

because men believe they are not seen
are not in God's presence when they judge

(even with their hands laid upon bibles
their interest devout self-interest)

and when we are tormented for being different
by laws of idol or human supremacy

his justice is brutally mocked
he has not desired it:

M E M

His own creation abandoning him
is a horror

but men can say and do as they want
they can act like gods: speak and it comes to pass

but they become heartless idols speaking
they will pass into dust and silence

they couldn't have opened their eyes
if the Lord did not desire it

and they strut in iron over us
yet the Lord does not will it—

because the words for good and evil
both came from him

NUN

We the living have a complaint
ignorance

a strong man or woman remembers
their weakness

instead of running from the past
turn to face the source

open your heart on the rough path of knowing
open your mind on the hard road of understanding

the solid ground supports
firm trust

let us search our ways
examine the difficulties within:

SAMECH

Where the will and faith turn bitter
repent that loss, return to him

take your heart in your hands
lift it high

sweetness flows from a broken heart
to heaven

we have hurt and destroyed
in self-righteous ignorance

Lord, we were lost in clouds of our own making
you could not forgive this

you knocked us down
you exposed us to your anger:

PEY

You were hidden behind it
we were slaughtered without mercy

the earth was a vast pen for us
you were hidden beyond the clouds

our prayers were hollow echoes
our hopes were crushed flowers

littering the ground like discolored pages
ripped from prayer books

you had made us garbage
in the world's eyes

human refuse
reeking in a senseless world

AYEN

Our misery only enraged them
all our enemies gathered to jeer us

we were beaten as a whining dog
our blood pounded in our ears

their mouths were opened wide
pouring our hatred

the world in open chorus
blind and shameless

we had fallen into a hole
the world was a hunter's pit

death was our horizon
terror as far as our eyes could see

T·Z·A·D·D·I·K

A dam burst in my eyes
to see the heart of my people broken

the daughter of my people terrorized
her defenses breached, pride swept away

all the built-up pressure released
like a river that runs forever

until the Lord looks down
to me

what I see with my own eyes
floods my mind, sickens me

I am swept up in the wake
of my daughter's despair

Q O P H

I was brought down for no reason
like a bird with a stone

by people who hate me just for being
again they bring me down, again

I am thrown into a pit
a stone is rolled over me

I who sing to the sky
am not to breathe

the nations of the world were like water
flowing over my head

to whom could I turn
I said to myself "I am gone"

RESH

In the deepest pit, Lord
I was drowning, alone

in the depths of abandonment
yet your name was on my lips

and you knew I was there
do not turn your ear from my groaning

whenever I turned to prayer
I felt you suddenly near

as if you said "do not fear"
Lord, you restored my soul

you were there and I knew
I could never be disowned

SHIN

You gave me the right to be myself
and you've seen men take it away

you've seen the hands across my mouth
Lord, speak for me and clear my name

even words have been subverted
I was brought to the bar of injustice

you saw their barbarous vengeance
you saw their final solution

my life was a living death
I was butchered for you

my death was the solution to all their problems
all their imagination was brought to my dying

T A U F

You heard their hatred crafted against me
as shameless as daily prayers

holy alliances condemning me
you saw the papers drawn up openly

their minds and their mouths fastened on me
like bloodsuckers

behind my back or in their company
I was spittle on their lips

in conference or on the street
I am the scapegoat uniting them

I lighten their labors
I am the guinea pig of their salvation

.   .   .

For the hands they raise to slaughter us
with your hand, Lord, strike them deeply within

let their pride be the poison they swallow
their hearts are stones, their minds tombstones

etched there forever let all their words mock them
with their bloody thoughts spilling into silent dust.

.   .   .

(Chapter 3)

Maccabees

THESE POEMS are found in *I Maccabees* and the scholarly evidence suggests they were written in the second century B.C., at least a generation before the book was edited. The narrative style of the book parallels the older books of Samuel and Kings, and the Maccabean psalms are likewise written in the style of the older *Psalms*. The attributions to Mattathias and Judah appear to be added by the editors, in order to weave the poems into the narrative; at the same time, the poets' names would have been expunged.

The authors were accomplished poets who probably had also written in Greek, prior to the plundering of Jerusalem; even when they wrote in Hebrew they had at one time assimilated the prevalent Hellenistic styles. Now, as the Maccabean dynasty arose, these poets returned to uniquely Hebraic forms, as their psalms make evident.

The Hebrew originals have been lost but a Jewish translation into Greek was made at the time, for use by the large Jewish population living in Alexandria and other Hellenistic cultures, including Judea. As these Jewish communities were transformed in character by the Roman Empire, and as Judeo-Greek died out, the Greek version was kept intact by the early Christian church. However, in place of the original Hebrew text, the books of the Maccabees were recalled by Jewish poets in the form of didactic Hebrew adaptations and poems, such as the medieval *Scroll of Antiochus*.

Early in the twentieth century, Abraham Kahana, a Jerusalem scholar, retranslated the Judeo-Greek version into Hebrew, imagining the text as it might have been composed. I consulted Kahana's Hebrew version.

❧ Maccabees ❧

A PSALM OF MATTATHIAS

Did I have to be born
raised to be a witness
to Jerusalem taken like a whore

my people massacred in spirit
sitting propped up like dead men
watching their city fall as if at a play

a foreign theater
at which they do not understand the language
but see their Temple stripped before their eyes

naked in the hands of enemies
and the audience disrobed: by the eyes
blind to their shame

sitting at a dumbshow
as if shy before the beauty
of their heritage

the very vessels
of the House
of Israel

paraded before them
in the hands of thieves
carried off into dark exile

and Israel watches
as her babes are killed in their mothers' arms
her young men slain over their books

in her streets and in her squares
again the curtain rises
another nation plays the conqueror

like many have done before it
having their way with her
leaving her stripped of personal possessions

she was a beautiful free woman
that now is left a slave
look, open your eyes

the Temple is empty
that was the vision of beauty
the glory in our lives

the spirit ripped from our chests—
do we just lean back
and go on living?

(2:7–13)

A P S A L M   O F   M A T T A T H I A S

There is no need for fear
of men dressed in threats of power
all their successes are masks

that will fade like words in a gust of wind
and though one walks as if he wears a crown
in a show of pride—the whole performance collapses

in an instant: one last breath
and his body crowns the dunghill
and his words have turned to worms

today he shines on everyone's tongue
tomorrow no one has heard of him
he's vanished quickly as a winter sunset

gone—turned back into dust
all his schemes turned back
into nothing

but you, my children, take hold of your lives
by a stronger hand
by the deep strength in Torah

your hearts unsinkable vessels
bearing its words: sustenance
for a day beyond mere dreams of success

it will bring you into the future
it will bring you courage
worn as surely as a crown.

(2:62–64)

A PSALM OF JUDAH

Jerusalem was a desert
empty of its spirit
none of her children were left

who had been signs of life
and none would go in
even Jerusalem air so pure

seemed choked with dust
the spirit that once breathed deeply
beheaded

the Temple quiet as a graveyard
walked upon by foreigners
as if it were grass

strangers were sleeping in the citadel
another desolate renovation
by pagans

Jacob awoke in a nightmare
and his children had gone
joy had abandoned him

flute and lyre
pipe and zither
had ceased.

(3:45)

A P S A L M O F J U D A H

When Judah saw how huge the enemy expedition was, he
prayed:

You are deeply felt
Lord beyond lords
Israel's strength is with you

who broke the spirit of warriors
crushing their plans along with their violent hero
by the hand of David, your servant

and the power of the Philistine army was dismantled
falling into the hand
of Jonathan, son of Saul—

in the same way, dismay this army
by the hand of Israel
humble their pride in superior number and horses

let their hearts be crushed by shame
let them be struck by panic
their arrogance melt away

let them quake in their boots
and run away in fear of destruction
by a people who love you

and let all who feel the power
behind your name which is a shield
feel like singing psalms to you.

(4:30–33)

Job

THE POET who composed *Job,* probably in the seventh century B.C. according to scholarly evidence, based it on an old legend. Embedded in the brief prose tale that frames the book, the legend tells what happens to a man in the grip of a terrible fate. Yet the poet of *Job* twists the legend with much irony, so that when Job finally submits to his fate he's rewarded with a better life.

A greater irony is that this is not a book about submission at all, since the poem that takes over the text refuses to submit—it rages against the indifference of fate. Job can't imagine that God would be indifferent, and in his stubborn zeal for the truth, Job is made Jewish by the Hebrew poet, unconsciously venting the most unconventional blasphemies.

The poem is cast in the form of a dialogue between Job and his friends. They advise him to accept his fate, suggesting ways to rescue his diginity. Job will not resign. In the end, God becomes a character wrapped in a whirlwind, intimidating Job into resignation. Even in this scene, and in the framing scene where God sits in his celestial court, Job is the truer character. The poet presents a caricature of God as a representation for conventional religion in his day: He lacks a human range of emotions. But one thing the character of God does not lack is a sense of irony; Job is the one who appears to be badly in need of it.

But Job's own words, as they reject irony—refusing to distance himself from pain—become an ironic triumph. How can we possibly live unless we hide some of our feelings? Job refuses the question; yet, in fact, he uses language and poetry gloriously—the very language that normally helps to sublimate feelings. In the character of Job, the Hebrew poet gives us a powerful portrait of a man divided against himself by language. Except for the tragicomedy of Jonah, it would take two thousand years for Job to be rivaled, in *Hamlet.*

Both Job and Hamlet listen to themselves as they speak. The Hebrew poet lets the irony of Job's speeches comment on themselves, while Hamlet comments directly. The framing comments of God in *Job* and Horatio in *Hamlet* serve to draw further attention to the verbal gifts of the protagonists, Job and Hamlet.

I focused on Job's speeches, the heart of the book. The summation of contemporary thought in the friends' speeches suggests that the Hebrew poet enlarged his poem at different times in his life, making the complete *Job* his life's work, as *Leaves of Grass* was Whitman's.

Most acutely in the words of Job, the poet drew upon popular proverbial expressions for irony, and I've consciously used the occasional cliché and idiom of popular culture for similar counterpoint. Our airwaves are just as filled with contending superstition and folklore (disguised as commercials or propaganda) as were the newsbearers of the ancient Middle East. Like many of the biblical poets, the poet of *Job* was a master of the satiric use of officialese.

In search of an English equivalent to the complex illusion of spokenness in Job's speeches, I found it in American poetry's struggle with natural speech, especially as it absorbed the influences of jazz composition. The shifts and changes in the flow of ordinary conversation, the often surreal collage of overheard imagery, heightens the sense of timing in the ear of the jazz musician–poet, who composes as he performs. John Coltrane said, "You got to keep talking/ to be real." I feel the quotation is apt for the character of Job.

CHAPTER 3

Rip up the day I was born
and the night that furnished a bed
with people to make me

the pillow from every night I lived
smother that day   cover its light
so God can forget it

let death's shadow
hold the ether mask there
clouds obliterate it

a total eclipse
blackout
swallow it a tiny pill

and that sweat that night beginning me
black oil absorb it
a hole drilled deep in calendars

shrivel that night in the hand of history
let it soften in impotence
turn off its little shouts of pleasure

every science unsex it
genetic biology   advanced psychology
nuclear bomb

no next morning shine on it
through the afterglow
singeing the eyelids of dawn

because it didn't shut the door
of the womb on me
to hide my eyes from pain

why couldn't I have been
a lucky abortion
why were there two knees

waiting for me
two breasts to suck
without them I could have stayed asleep

I could have melted away
like spilled semen
in transparent air

wrapped up in quiet dust
with gods of power and influence
and the emptiness of their palaces

with rich families their money
paper houses
for plastic children

with criminals who can't break loose
there they rest with tired workers
no more hell from bosses or jailers

who all fall down
under one blanket
not the simplest machine to serve them

why should someone have to live
locked in a miserable spotlight
bitter inside

waiting for a death far off
they search for it restlessly
like the final person in a late-night bar

they can't wait to see the iron gate unlock
and the little grave plot
comforts them

why should someone have to walk around
blinded by the daylight
he can't wave off

that God throws on him
waiting at every exit
in front of me

a table of sighs to eat
and moaning
poured out like water

every horror I imagined
walks right up to me
no privacy no solitude

and my pain
with my mind
pushes rest aside.

CHAPTER 6

Weigh my anguish
heave my misery on that scale
heavier than a planet

a scale filled with sand
that's how words fail me
God's arrows spinning past me

poisoning my spirit
wearing me away
little petty arguments

would you like only egg whites
no salt to season
every meal

the soul blanches
dizzy at the sight
of my own white flesh

I hope God will change this prayer
white paper hope
to violence of reality

crush me
snip off my life
paper

what a relief
I'd leap with delight
that departing train of pain

knowing I broke no law
but where to get some strength to wait
cold patience

a head of stone
skin of metal
nerves frozen dead

no help from inside
I can't reach in there
anymore

sick spirit
my dear friends
disappearing frightened nurses

and snow falls
over mouths of pure water
hidden high in mountains

of themselves
sheer ice cliffs
face my simple thirst

spring comes
they dry up
fast as a mirage

caravans lost
looking for what they thought
new roads

new places
fresh faces
tricked

by nature's technology
human nature's
idiocy

and that's how you look at me friends
panicked
into your empty words

do I say give me
things or money
save me from enemy

pay my dues for me
so talk straight I listen
at my open mistake

honesty so easy to take
but not the "advice"
unsheathed metal

to pain me with words
and deaf to mine
the wind blows away

do you lecture disaster victims
high-pressure a friend
stab love full of arguments

now look at me
face into face
no place here to glibly hide

think again—your thinking stopped
as in a blind spot
you passed my integrity

my face wide open
as I speak
my tongue there true

not as if I couldn't taste
bitter fruit
my words in my mouth.

We're all somebody's workers
in a big factory
grasping for breaks

reaching for paychecks and prizes
here I'm paid these empty months
heavy nights awarded

to lie down and wait
for getting up
dragged through toss and turnings

body dressed in a texture of scars
little white worms of skin
while days run on smoothly

through a tape recorder
to run out
beyond machine of hope

mouth making a little wind
eyes straining harder
to finally disappear

in front of others' eyes
as clouds breaking up
we fall beneath the ground

we don't go home again
house doesn't know me
so nothing holds me back here

listen to this mind in pain
this "educated" soul
in words it complains

am I some Frankenstein
to be guarded
can't go to sleep alone

find some dream waiting
to terrify me
break my neck

only to find it there again
why not a hand instead
to really choke me

shake hands with despair friends
I have all day
it's all one little breath

so leave me alone God
why think up a man
think so much of one

to open it for inspection
every morning
test it every breath

look over there
somewhere other
give me just one free moment

to swallow my spit
what did I do to hurt you
man watcher

what can you be making
what cosmic thought
I'm necessary for

you hold me here
insignificant comma
like a tie in a railroad track

why not forgive
forget
I'll just settle down in dust here

you won't have to think
to even look
for me.

CHAPTER 9

However true
we don't know how to win a case
against God

for every question we'd ask
there are a thousand
over our heads

however high and headstrong
who among us   heart of stone
is hard enough to resist him

he picks up a mountain
it doesn't even know it
and throws it down

when he's angry
he gives the earth a little kick
and it trembles

he brews up a storm
to hide the sun
erase the stars

he laid the universe out
on the blackboard of space
alone with himself

he paced up and down
thinking something
that charmed the primitive sea

his thoughts clear as stars
laid on the surface
of a calm sea

he passes by
and we don't see him
as our heads swell with impressions

each day
sometimes bitter
we'd say "wait, wait a minute,

what are you doing?"
but he has passed us
long ago

all the gods of human history
couldn't raise a whisper
to slow him down

so what could I say
to turn him
around

even if I'm right
even if he heard
a little murmur of human truth

it would only be irritating
stopping him for even a moment
he'd knock the breath out of me

as he brushed
a fleck of soot
or tear from his eyes

(he is the means
to make justice
his end)

I could be right
and my mouth
would say something wrong

totally innocent
and my words
wrap around me

in a cloak of pride
but I'm innocent
I don't care about myself

I don't know my life
as if it makes any difference
we're all destroyed together

guilty   not guilty
some disaster strikes
mixing innocence with despair

and someone is laughing at his experiment
the whole world is wrapped
in a cloak of pride

like a prize scientist
of pride   white and clean
it's all a desperate show

the faces of our judges are covered
with the gauze
for this human play

and he made it   you
who can prove
I'm a liar

my days print out
faster than a computer
they're gone like Western Union boys

fleeing from the horror
of "progress"
exploded bombs

if I say
I'll put on a happy face
grit my teeth grin and bear it

some inner torture takes over
every time   I can hardly believe it
you'll never let me go!

my life is a sentence
why should I struggle
in these chains of words

I could wash my mouth with soap
my hands in lye
and you'd drop me into some ditch

and I'd fall on my face
until I couldn't even laugh
or challenge his force

I'd hate myself
as if all my clothes
turned into prisoner's clothes

he isn't a man
with a hand to put a summons in
was I ever in a court

can my mind come up with a court
some kind of referee or witness
to step between us

let him put down that club
that terror of naked space
he holds over me

then I could find myself
put on consciousness openly
but he won't let me be.

CHAPTER 10

My soul is sick of life
pushes me to speak
to fill the air with wounds

don't leave me hanging God
let me see the case
against me   is there honor

just to cut me down
to think so little of the work
that flowed from your hands

that you sit back watching the mean
arrogantly misshapen
bask in the spotlight

and can you see through the tiny eyes of men
eyes of flesh
in the little prism of a day

are your years our years
that you make me suffer in
that you enter to turn upside down

though you only you know I'm guiltless
where could I escape
beneath your hand

hands that molded me alive
and now reach in to crush me—
remember the mud you cupped for me

it's only the same dust I can return to
the dust on the bottle of milk
you poured me out of

worked me up into something solid
like rich cheese
wrapped in a beautiful skin

and inside the dream architecture of bones
you filled me with breath and vision
a vision of reality a love

but you cloud these things in a mind
of your own
a sky I know the stars stretch back from

containing all time forever
you surround me with clouds
like a lens

to see if I will
with this little mirror of a mind
think I can escape

cloud myself in nerve
and if I do—God help me
and if I'm innocent I better not look up

drunk with shame
drenched in this misery
of myself

if I stand up you come to me
cold as a camera
your pictures are marvelous pictures

they multiply your anger toward me
frame after frame
an army of moments against me

why did you pull me through the womb
locked into the brutal focus of time
I could have died inside never breathed

no one come to look at me
a quick blur in the world
carried stillborn from womb to tomb

so few days this life
why not just leave me alone
let me smile a little while

before I go off never to return
into the deep shadow of death
utter darkness—the thing itself

stripped of the background darkness
into the flaming
sun of darkness.

CHAPTER 12

Of course you're all so cultured
when you die (what a loss)
wisdom dies with you

but I have a mind too
working just like yours
who doesn't anyway?

yet you come by almost laughing
at a man who called out God
and was answered

and in that innocence
I'm an idiot in a showcase
for all those comfortably hidden

in the things they've accumulated
a sideshow in a pit
for you thinking you're not trapped

looking down on me as if I'd slipped
out of weakness   out of love
for an immaterial illusion

a dreamy escape
while thieves pile up things in their houses   any man
sneers behind his mask at God

secure in his heartless estate
anything his hand can grab onto
is god enough for him

look at his dog or cat
and think where they came from
the pigeons flocking in the park will tell you

look at the ground and it will tell you
with the flowers on its blanket
covering over ages of living things

fish in the sea will speak to you
as you have to me bloated with words
you mouth as if you've learned

learned to mouth without feeling
we all everything swim from God's hand
everything we make with our hands

he put in front of us
and in time ahead of us
as we begin from little fish with tails

don't our mouths know what food is
and what tastes foreign
as our ears know what words

swim to the heart
does it matter how long we've lived
do we pile up wisdom in our nets

or do we dip them again every day in the river
because wisdom flows only from God
he feeds the mind

if he breaks a living thing apart
we can't rebuild it
if he shuts the door on a man

there is nothing there to open
no rain and the earth dries up
he lets the water loose we're immersed

he's the source of energy and reflection: wisdom
the power-mad and the slave
dissolve to the same source dissolve in the mirror

and if he wishes
the wise are stripped of their wisdom
judges go mad in their courtrooms

the belt of power slips from the wearer
clothes don't fit them
like poor men in mental wards

priests are stripped and led away
money slips through the hands of the rich
like water

those most full of confidence
lose their voices
men we trust lose their senses

heirs and those next in line
have contempt poured on their heads
mantles of power shrink out of shape

the muscles of strongmen are water—
death plots spawned in the dark
are totally exposed

like negatives to light
death's shadow is immersed
in light

he swells nations to greatness
then deflates them
a nation is swept off its feet

the minds of its leaders are blown away
scattered like old newspapers
blown through a cemetery

they grope for some kind of light switch
in an ancient tomb
they flail like men overboard

drunk on their own power
they stagger toward a caved-in door
in some ancient bar.

CHAPTER 13

My eye has seen it
my ear heard and grasped
the vision

I know what you know
nothing less
than you

so I'd speak to God
to the one
whose reason is all

you are all plasterers
you think you are doctors
but it's only broken walls before you

you smear them over
with a whiteness of lies
a color you take for truth itself

you should shut up before them
and your silence become
a road to wisdom

stop then on your way
here on these lips
is a little plea

you speak for God
and in that acting
you can only be false

you have a case amorphous as air
the court is only a conceit
behind your forehead

what can you say
when you catch him
in a lie or contradiction

will you make him squirm
can you make him speechless
in his witness?

his words will unmask you
your conceit crack and fade
like a painted smile of piety

you will crack in the sun
of his majesty and fall
to pieces before him

your heavy talk in the dust
of ashes
with the clean little homilies

the niceties broken like clay
lay there then in your dumbness
so I may speak

opening to whatever
becomes
of me

my flesh may become
the one last meal
in my mouth

my breath become
the one last drink
in my hand

though he slay me
yet these words stand
to speak up

to his face
they are my voice itself
no false witness

could find these words
you see I'm not cut off
stand back   listen

to the voice of poetry
that is making my case
and may be lasting justice itself!

who else is there
to argue with this song
cut the air out of my life

then I'd rest content with silence
death sentence
but still two things more

I ask of you
to allow me to open
myself in your eyes

remove the hand that falls
leaden on me
like a heavy depression

except that I move   falls
like silent terror
except that I speak

and lighten my fear
I want to walk out of the dark
to meet your fierce stare

call me and I'll be there
just as right now I'm speaking
for you to answer here

how many crimes and untold lies
am I unconscious of
how can I see them

with your face hidden
veiled in silence
what enemy is in me

that you squeeze in a vise
but at such distance
infinite space

am I a leaf spun away
in a burst of wind
impossible to see

what power in that leaf
blindly afloat
to feel terror

this numb piece of paper
you squeeze my feelings on
held in this painful air:

bitter words
you have written down
against me

a list I inherit
from the unspoken lies
of my past

my feet are also locked
as if you would hold me
ready for punishment

in that vise
some crime some slight
some monstrous pinprick

forced you to look
narrowly at me
narrowing my path

noting each unique footprint
brand of a slave
a voice singing out through the bars.

CHAPTER 1 4

Man swims out of a woman
for a few days of restless living
full of anxieties

a flower springing up
under the passing cut
of the share's thrust

a shadow fading out
of time
gone

disintegrating
like an old wineskin
an old coat

eaten away
by moths
drained

and this is the creature
you open your eyes on
take time to judge

as if pure earth can be extracted
out of lust-spattered hair
by a man himself

however young or innocent
he dies
in a dusty coat of experience

because our days are numbered
so we can count them ourselves!
approximate the whole

short story
you give us
with its "The End"

look the other way   turn your eyes away
why don't you
just let us be here

ignorant slaves
enjoying our work
enjoying our sleep

till we finish this simple story
and get a little rest . . .
even a tree cut down

has some hope
it can spring to life
old roots

start up tenderly
even if its body stump
dies in the dust

soon as it whiffs some water
it starts
growing like a new plant

but a man just disappears
one last breath
and where is he

lakes have completely evaporated
rivers shrunk away
and men laid down to rest

never to rise
or materialize
the sun can die

galaxy collapse
space evaporate
universe shrink to a ball

and we will not hear it
nothing will shake us
awake in our beds

if only you could hide me
beyond existence
outside of space and time

in a darkness
a secret
beyond the known

until your famous anger passes
and then you remember me
waiting for the book to close

waiting for an appointment!
is it just possible
a man dies and lives again?

I'd bear any day   every day
heavy as it is
waiting

for your call
and I would answer
you want to hear me again

this creature you made with care
to speak
to you

but now you number each step I take
note so slight a false movement
I can't even see it

as if my guilt is sealed
under a coat of whitewash
faded from my eyes but there

as a mountain
that will finally fall
a rock that will be moved

a rain wearing away the stone
a storm a flood
washing the earth away

as you wash away
the hopes of a man
we are lost at sea

our faces go blank
unrecognizable
painted out forever

sunk out of your sight
we swam a little
and we drowned

our families rise in the world
we don't know them
or they fall

or they disgrace themselves
sink into despair
we don't think of them

we only feel our own flesh
rotting   only hear
the echo of our body:

the pains of its dying,
the mourning
of its self.

CHAPTER 16

I've heard these righteous clichés
over and over
thanks for the precious comfort

the heavy breathing
in a bag of wind
that just gets noisier

you want to drown me out
with monotonous whispering
platitudes?

I could do that if I were you
like putting any word in front of the next
while making faces at a baby

the tone is one of a sermon
you solemnly deliver
with just the right voice quiver

babble on
till the baby falls asleep
but when I really speak

my pain stays there
and if I hold myself back
I'm still alone with it

and him
his famous jealousy
wearing me down

like precious jewelry
over my entire body like skin
each minute becomes heavier

I'm distracted by myself
alienating all my company
who turn on me

like bribed witnesses—
the friends I counted on!—
lying into my face

friends who've disappeared
like flesh on my body
thinned by tension

wrinkled by despair
slim enough to be accused
as I'm barely standing

of paranoia or hunger
therefore craving bread
therefore a liar to myself

whose open face
hides these hot words
steaming in my mouth

but it's clear I'm consumed
on the flame of his anger
in the gnashing of teeth

in the eyes that flash
sirens across my face
the mouth that curls in a snarl

an arm reaches out a claw
slaps my face
my friends become a mob a beast

with the faceless energy called courage
of a bitten animal
raw violence

selfish masks
ripped away from the unconscious
faceless the way they really are

and I'm delivered
by my God
to this transparent world

of bitter losses vicious plots
covered with a veneer
of paper thin consciousness

the masks of sincerity
dropped like hot coals
in God's rage against me

I was content
happy productive peace-loving
peace-making

until he grabbed me by the neck
spun me around
and shattered me

worried me to pieces
pulled me together a moment
to stand as a target

for friends and enemies
what's the difference
I could be them

blindly righteous
strangers to ourselves
we think our eyes are friends

confidently looking out for us
but they'd close in the instant
they saw the volcano within

the first volcano
and when we turn to look back at the world again
it's almost too dim to see

slowly we adjust to the light in the room
this is the world we're made for
but where is the human light

of justice coming from—through the crack
within   or from without
but space is all the same

and on both sides I'm a target
God's arrows spinning past me
his men surround me

and I'm hit
again and again
piercing my stomach my bowels

spilling my insides out
he clubs me down
leader of the riot

or the purge the pogrom
he is a policeman
and I am wearing rags

can't change my clothes
can't shave can't move
my life my plans paralyzed

till my head sinks into dust
heavy antlers
of a battered wild ram

humiliation
my face a red desert
from weeping

craters of depression
the dark eye shadow
of death

and not a drop or speck
of violence
from my own hands

not a bad wish
not a curse in the cleanness
of my daily creations

O earth, cover not over my blood!
don't be a tomb a museum
for my miserable poem

my cry against this sinking
leave my voice uncovered
a little scar on your face

face of the earth
open to the sky
the universe

where you can see
a justice waiting to be discovered
like an inner referee

the deep seat of conscience
where a creator sits
handing me these words themselves

these verses are my absolving witness
on this little home earth
from which they speed

out into the universe forever!
even as my tears
fall in the dust

before an angry God who hears and sees
my plea   words and tears
of a man

for the life of his brother or son
the love of another living man
who is also me

on the outside
and inside the listening unconscious
creator who is also he

as clear as the clearest dream
as the little ball of earth
seen in a photograph

whom I call with my breath
as if he were human
unlike these words living beyond me

for I know I'm sentenced to die
my little story of years
will soon be over

I'll be going down the road
to fall in the dust
just one time.

CHAPTER 17

My breath straining
my days fading
through a prism of pain

in my chest
thinning my voice my hair
getting me in shape

for the grave
surrounded by a chorus
of mockingbirds

who won't let me rest
my eyes wide open
on the hard bed

of their bitterness . . .
lay down something beside me
some collateral I can grasp

you yourself
granted me this speaking
no one else will back me

no one shakes this open hand
you've closed their minds
shrunk their hearts into a bird's breast

but you won't let them sing
over me   in the morning
because they're shut in their ignorant night

denying a friend
for some self-righteous flattery
precious blinders for their eyes

while their children's sight grows dim
who recognize my famous name
trademark for bad medicine

something to spit at the feet of
my eyes are also blurred
but by tears

my hands and feet
fading away
like shadows

if any man is really open
he'll stop in his tracks
at this trial

of standing up
on innocent feet
among brothers

and being covered with total abuse
still that man will walk on
through the heap of civilized refuse

the wasteland of clichés
spiritual materialism
and his legs will grow stronger

meanwhile the show goes on
men of the world
stone me

with the ready-made knowledge
any idiot can buy in the supermarket
my business totally collapsing

my days fading like an echo
of the shattering
of my ego   all my plans

my heartstrings
cut silently
in the night that switches to day

at the push of a button
like the unconscious habit
of false righteousness

taking the powers that be
for granted
and so I can't even sleep

you come to me with these rigid proverbs
these artificial lights
like "there's light at the end of the tunnel"

all I want to see is reality
of darkness   to make my bed
underground

grave you are my father!
worm my mother
and my sisters

so here I am in the dust
faithfully returned to
so this is the hope

I should bow down to?
where are we then
but in the fading light of the unconscious

turning dreams to lost memories
dreams of a decent life
who can see anyone else's   _but him_

the innocence of them
spontaneous trust
my spirit open to them

will they also go down with me and with
these dream mouths of friends
to the ancient bar of dust

the vast unconscious cellar
to become dry bones
all my dreams of a livable future.

CHAPTER 1 9

How long does this gale
of words go on
this wind

you turn on my spirit
choking me
each time you've opened your mouths

is an insult friends
a hot brand on me
cast-iron reproductions of advice

meant for sheep
it doesn't offend you
to goad me like one

let's say I did something wrong
it's none of your business
no example for your self-righteous

spiritual merchandise
the goods making you feel superior
as if this rag of skin is proof

of my poverty
open your ears your silk purses
a minute: it's God who's

done me wrong
this chain around my neck
is not my words or thoughts

if I cry help
I'm being strangled
no one can hear

where's the judge
to hear these groans
from a poor man

I'm locked in my own ghetto
the streets are dimmed
by walls of pain

my pride stripped away
my humble crown of faith
in my own work and spirit

knocked down
my body a truth horribly distorted
I'm nothing

torn down like an old building
gone before you know it
a vacant lot

paved over
not even the hope of a tree
my smallest hope makes him angry

kindling for his rage
I'm the enemy
surrounded by his troops

with your ironclad masterplan
cut off the city
as if I were some Leningrad

but my brothers are far away
removed   remote
my friends totally aloof

relatives don't know me
my closest friends
don't remember who I am

guests in my house
never knew me
to neighbors I'm the worst kind of stranger

an immigrant a beggar a bum
in the eyes of women I supported
invisible to men who worked for me

even when I ask them humbly
as a poor dog
a few tender yelps

an intimate embrace a kiss
fills my wife with horror
just the smell of my breath

my whole family is disgusted
backing off
coughing in disgust

children on the street
hold their noses   spit
run from me

all my deepest friends turn away
can't stand the sight of me
all those I loved the best

my bones creak laughing at me
my skin loose around them
like toothless gums   leprous

my teeth disappearing
there's hardly one left or anything solid
holding me together

some pity friends a little pity
dear friends
I'm wounded   struck

by the hand of God
a serious blow you can see
why do you keep on hurting me

why is the pleasure of my flesh not enough
that you need to squeeze
the last breath from my spirit

Oh if only these words were written down
printed and reproduced
in a book

engraved carved
with an iron pen
into solid rock forever!

monumental inscription
filled with volcanic lead
hardened into my one solid witness!

but inside myself
I know my witness breathes
to answer me   God himself

giving birth to words
vision itself
my constant creator

an answering wind like out of my mouth
to turn my case around
in front of the world

my judge and referee
and I'll be there
even without my flesh

though cancer devours my skin
I'll stand up   behind this body
my spirit will somehow pull me up

even for a moment to see it
in the twinkling of an eye
through the open window

of my own eyes
still alive
my living heart feeling

the justice of his presence
beside me within me
before I die

as I almost did
when you joined the bandwagon
of my pain

waving at me to stop
as if it was all my fault
as if I started the engine

but you'll stop at a whistle friends
that blows you down
that blows your spiritual arrogance away

the sound of your own pain
opening your eyes
to a higher judgment.

CHAPTER 21

Just listen to me
you're all sealed up
in the big consolation

of blind faith
that you offer me so generously
but if you'd just open a little hole

in your ears
I'd be happy enough being alive
speaking these words to living beings

then you can resume mocking
anyway it's not you not men
pushed me to voice my thinking

to have to speak my mind
total consciousness
to listen to my own self calling

to hear all and nothing
the answer in the call
more than one man can stand

so what good is patience
look at me head-on
and be amazed

as your hand jumps
to cover your mouth
gaping astonished

when I stop to think
myself
I'm paralyzed

my skin crawls
pure horror
here it is   hear it

why do totally corrupted men
go on living
grow old in style

grow richer every day
see their children grow
into their power and houses

in safety   insured
peace to them
and their brothers

God's arrows
don't reach them
no heavy justice for them

their bulls mount their cows
no sooner said than done
a calf without fail

they have a flock of children
frisky little lambs
they run out to play

and dance to the tambourine
and sing with the lyre
and absorb the melody of flutes

their lives close like a sunset
prosperous and peaceful
they head to the grave

go down softly under
and yet
they'd said to God

leave us alone
we don't want to know
of you

why do we need God
to be servants
and what's there to get

from meditating on it
what's the profit
in spending our time on him?

isn't their happiness
in their own hands
isn't this circle of corruption

outside God's orbit
as you think of the unscrupulous
do you see their lights

turned off
their careers in ruins
bodies struck by heavy hand

because God is mad at them?
how often
and do you see them turned

to rags
yesterday's newspaper
blowing in the wind

you say his children
will end up paying for it?
no—let his own nerves

strain for the price
his own eyes
see himself break down

a shattered mirror
blown apart
in a heavy wind

let him live and learn
and drink from the cup
that's thrown in his face

what does he know or care
how his house stands
like a man totally drunk

he's finished the bottle
of his life
died satisfied

is there something God should learn
from us
here

something about spiritual materialism
the debt he owes and forgot
to pay the corrupt and yes the self-righteous

because you yourselves
become his judge
when you write off the reality

of the world he made
set in front of you
just as it is

one man dies at a healthy age
drinking to the full
his milk pails were always full

marrow of his bones still sweet
body still attractive
to women   attracted by them

and another man dies shrunken
in a bitter spirit
not even a drop of happiness

and then they lie down together
in the same bed of dust
with worms to cover them up

and yes I know your thoughts
the wooden arguments
the corpses you're lining up

you want to ask your rigid questions
but where *is* Stalin's house now
or Franco's

not to mention countless
run of the mill criminals
never caught: Martin Bormann etc.

the loyal collaborators
the rich and privileged saluting
any flag that flies their way

reflected in the polished boots of chauffeurs
Mercedes-Benz
certain popes

and busy in the wings the faceless
you won't see them standing around
at any apocalypse

you ought to ask some tourists
who speak your language
open-mindedly

listen to some impartial camera clicks
look at the photographs
even postage stamps

you push me into irony
and out the other side
to common sense

the deeply corrupt disappear
in limousines and passports
flown to obscure small towns

or islands
relax or even return
after the dust settles

and newspapers have crumbled
no one stings him with pointed proverbs
under his beard

no one unmasks him face to face
he lives like a god
and dies on the shoulders

of the mass of dupes
who carry him to his grave
which becomes a protected museum

his mouth is fixed at peace
by the embalmer   the priest
throws no dirt on his reputation

he'll live in some history
while the masses supporting him
are barely a footnote

Hollywood extras
following the hearse
lining the curbs

why this empty comfort you point to
these empty nothings you argue
this empty room of thought

you goad and push me into
this dark and hostile consolation
this humorless nonsense of empty religion.

CHAPTER 23

Today again
my speech my poem
this hard-talking blues

this heavy hand
from the long deep writing
of my spirit

Oh if I could know
where to go
and there

find him
at home
in his seat of justice

I'd sit down there
to lay out my case
before him

my mouth would be full
like a river
of what my heart must say

my mind open
like a window
to hear his words

as easy to understand
as the sounds of people
on the street

I wouldn't be blown away
overpowered
by them

but my own voice would be steadied
like a tree outside
in a bracing March wind

wind between the wood
earthly music
stirring my spirit

in his house
where an upright open man
isn't afraid to confront him

to listen to respond
to contend   a human music
creating the air

for a higher justice
in which to hear
I'm set free

but now I look to the east
and he isn't there
west and a vast empty ocean

face north
like a true compass
see nothing

turn south
and he's still invisible
hidden from my ear

but he follows each step I take
even when I'm sitting doing nothing
and he puts me in the crucible

to have his gold
because I've walked all my life
toward his light

past the neon temptation
of unreal cities
surreal commercials for "normality"

my lips have opened
for his infinite word
in meditation

I've opened his book
in my heart
and read with open eyes

he is one
determined within himself
as end

and has an end
all changes all choices
rest in his mind

but how can I change his mind
his soul desires
and it's already been done

ancient history
past changing
beyond our time

here he hands me
part of a sentence
already out of his mouth

and there's more to say
just as the past fills
with more to discover

it makes me shiver
to think
I must face him

here on this earth
now in this life
present in the infinite

transfigured
as my inaccessible inner self
rises to his hand

I turn white
cold sweat of fear
washes across my face

I want to turn back
as if I'm walking in my sleep
out of a world I know

my own shadow
smiles back at me
a shadow in the night

the past is drunk with strangeness
and his presence
drowns my heart in naked space

because he brought me out here
into the darkness
where I must continue speaking

into the open
like a child holding tight
to the side of his trembling crib.

CHAPTER 2 4

The days of judgment
and everyone has one
are no dark secret

because God has finished his sentence
but men are mostly blind
and that's the way God made it

but why are his hearers
also deaf
to the coming of those days

while corrupted men
totally in the dark
cut through fences and honest agreements

and anyone in their way
knocking down the shepherd
stealing the sheep

they drive off
in the repossessed cars
of the poor

foreclose
on widows and orphans
lock up a workman's tools

shove the homeless
out of their way
terrorize old people

already cringing
in little groups
huddled in corners

and the masses
are exploited asses
donkeys up a mountain

or camels in the desert
they report for work
as they're told

as the sun rises until dark
carrying the water they can't take home
to their thirsty children

they harvest healthy food
for corrupt masters
pick the ripe grapes

for the cynical toasts
of the power-hungry
spilling the precious wine of their sweat

to finally lie down
naked under cold stars
not a shirt on their back

to wear in the predawn
dew from the mountains
making them roll over in their sleep

and hug close
a rock
shelter from the storm

when it rains
while the privileged few
snore in their yachts

on the sea of the masses
on the sweat of their backs
on the milk of a mother's breast

from whose arms they'd wring
the brief soft luxury
that's all most men ever know

rip the child
from the widow's breast
as security

against some calculated debt
to keep the heads of the poor
under water

in a sea of desperation
naked of human rights
a mass of mesmerized slaves

walking through the rich waves
of grain
bringing in the sheaves

for a perversely ornate table
half-starved
the workers of the world

between stones
pressing oil for the ruling classes
only their sweat belongs to them

treading the winepress of the bosses
in life's oasis
dying of thirst in the desert

listen to those distant groans
far from the drowning hum
of the city

a wounded army of souls
gasping in their ancient tracks
but God doesn't hear that prayer

and in the cities
even among the elite
men get away with murder

darkness meets darkness
a blood pact
against his light

light of day
of reality
of the inspiration for making

electric light
and the continuing surprise
of every morning sunrise

there are men
who've lost the path
to daylight

rising at daybreak
to terrorize the caravans
of the huddled masses

murderers
and at night under their dark blanket
thieves

adultery: another broken commandment
under cover of darkness
and masks

any form of disguise
a man in woman's clothes
slipping into the harem

thinking under his veil
no one will see me
no one know but she

they break up houses
as criminals
break into them

into the ones at night
they marked that day
in an ignorant scrawl of a mind

blind
to the light
we are given

strangers in the morning
to their own shadow
floating on the surface of consciousness

they are submerged
in the nightmare unconscious
because they can't make anything

of the light of a star
focused like a conscience
in the eye of imagination

creating light
in the image of light
honest day light

I rise from a dream in
to discover the universe without
that was within

rising past superstition
idols and dumb images
having nothing to say in daylight

yes belief requires dreams
and every night
we go to sleep in this world

while those others are at home
talking and listening
to shadows

completely intimate
with the nightmare
of death's shadow

show me
this isn't true
reduce these words to nothing

to nonsense like a magician
and I'll show you as your new servant
my eyes were fixed on reality.

CHAPTERS 26 – 27

Since I'm so weak
and this poem so pitiful
so powerless

I'm lucky again today
to have such friends
such care for the feeble

how nobly you've lifted
this poor arm that writes
what a miracle

what strong donations
you've made to little minds
barely subsisting on the minimum wisdom

I can hardly know what I'm saying
except thanks to you
your fatherly advice spilling over me

but who filled you with it
and who are you speaking to
what possesses you

to form such a rigid piety
with a breath
caught in what flow of meaning

my poem has a way
to continue
even as I swear by God

who holds back my living right
to be free of bitterness
that damn it I'm speaking

my own mind as he allows
as these breaths come out of me
these shreds of phrases

my spirit revives and hangs on
to the wind God sends
through my nostrils

and the words that leap off my lips
fall true to the page
of my conscience

it's out of my hands
to let you get away
with your self-righteous platitudes

as solid as flotsam
but as long as I'm alive
I won't let go

of the stone rightness
my spiritual individuality
until I die

the page of my heart
opens to the wind
of his warming breath

let my enemy be as cold
as the heartless
my accuser suffer

the secret death chills
of the liar
perspire with the guilty

cold sweat flow
in his veins
dripping from a heart as stiff

as an icicle   a conscience
upright but hopeless
as he prays

for what help
meditates on what
burning sphere of thought

that may give him a push
through the world of things to accumulate
but what is there to get

when his body loses its grasp
on life   does God hear
the cry of this hypocrite

will he delight in his calling
man to God   a dialogue
or has this man's words been smothered

behind a mask
yes I know something about it
God's place

inside us
moving my hand
that lifts and calls

to him
it has nothing to conceal
my mind is an open book

for God's hand
take a look
you must have read there

so why have you become so proud
you blow your hot empty breath
your stream of words on me.

CHAPTER 29

Who can turn me around
until I find myself
back in the old days

the good days
God watching over me
the sun shining

inside me
like inner light
to usher me past the nightmares

on the screen of giddy youth
my life was in focus
around me   it was autumn

wife and children growing
my walks were bathed in light
in cream

the heaviest rocks in my way
smoothed out
like oil

I was as if transported
wherever I went
on a stream of affection

when I went out the city gates
or when I came to my place
in the city square

the younger men quickly stepped
aside   like a wave disappearing
while the older men rose to their feet

celebrities stopped
in the middle of what they were saying
and almost covered their mouths

the voices of politicians trailed off
like old newspapers
blown in the wind

their tongues dried up
dusty leaves
swept to the back of their mouths

I mean men listened to me
you could hear a leaf drop
they wanted my opinion

when I finished I was allowed
the clarity of silence
my words fell gently on them

like spring rain
they were attentive as trees
opening their arms

stretching their hands out gladly
as if their minds were open
to the sky

and when I laughed or
made light of things
they were almost stunned

to be reminded I was human
their eyes would light up
blossoms the sun smiled on

I directed their thoughts
to the best way   a revelation
they followed like actors visibly

in the presence of a master
a man who'd paid more than his dues
inspiring confidence in the disillusioned

their ears would open
and mouths speak of me
graciously

anyone seeing me
became a witness
to my openness

I embraced a poor man
and an orphan
and a man with no one in the world

to turn to
a man dying gave me a blessing
a widow smiled with joy for me

I opened myself
and a cloak of pride
slid from my shoulders

I embraced a sense of justice
that wrapped itself around me
like a warm coat in winter

I was eyes to the blind
and feet
to the lame

a father to the homeless
a light in the midnight window
to the stranger far from home

I was a destroyer of nightmares
like a gentle counselor
in an orphanage

then I said to myself
I will die
in the open arms of a family

and my seed in that nest
outgrow the arithmetic of a lifetime
the calculations of a mind

or historical lineage
my spirit extends beyond time
like a phoenix rising

from ashes
an ancient poem
from the dust of pages

my roots reaching out
for water
each new coming spring

and the dew shall lie all night
on my branches
and I feel the sweetness of that weight

on me
that miraculous touch
of heaven

waking my heart
made light again
by the fire of love within

my pen returning to the page
like an arrow to the heart
a love as strong as death.

But now it's all a joke
to the younger generation
I'm an outdated ape

too heavy to take seriously
for the puppies of men
who in my time I wouldn't

have insulted my dogs by going near!
dogs whose hearts were higher
among my flocks of sheep

men whose hearts burned out
in a destruction of spirit
shriveling their humanity into rags

they haunt the back alleys
of a civilized wasteland
like the "disgusting" gypsies

they stooped to revile
in false images
to make themselves feel superior

devastated Indians
of their own manufactured
nightmares

eating the weeds
they claw up greedily
like outcast witches

banished from the self-righteous society
that rightly hounds them
like fleeing common criminals

they huddle in unblanketed pits
in primitive dreams: caves
of obsolete railroad cars

wallowing in the mud
of self-pity
gnawing the worms of desire

their sons a gang of animals
monsters of inhuman pride
hands on their belts like horsewhips

and now I've become the bait of their humor
their theme song
their saddle their fetish

their figure of contempt
they are primitive giants of ice
aloof over me

I'm the floor
they spit on
because God has knocked me down

unstrung the bow of my back
unleashed the curs
of their tongues on me

these vile witnesses at my right hand
this vigilante lynch mob
has come down my road of ruin

there are no living heroes
to step out of nowhere
in their way

all my defenses broken down
inevitably as water
breaks through an abandoned dam

my nerves on edge
wild deer fleeing
from the cracks of a thunderstorm

terror faces me like a wall
or a wind blowing my strength away
my hope disappearing like a cloud

my soul emptied like a glass of water
and in my hand
are miserable tears

my very bones are sweating
at night my veins
restlessly throb

my clothes and skin
bleached beyond recognition
by the acid of my suffering

my collar shrinks tight
around my throat
the hand of God's wrath

which drags me down to the mud
my spirit itself is dressed
in dust and ashes

I speak to you
hard and true
over the heads of men

who look down at me
my voice goes out of me
a wounded bird

flying to you
in your sky   crying
its whole being is calling

to you and you
don't answer
I stand trembling before you

and you look at me
as if I'm not there
as if you don't know or care

what I want
you sit in your great high chair
and in your great satisfaction

toy with me cruelly
your hand bears down on me
heavy and hostile

I'm like crumpled paper
lifted in your wind
driven to the edge of existence

tossed in a tempest
my significance dissolved
in the heavy downpour

without the warmth of your care
even the word significance
bleeds dry

I know your arm is leading me
to my death
to the meeting house

where every living creature
lies down
before you

but did I ever lift
my arm
to strike or sweep away

a ruined heap of a man
whose tortured voice reached out
for help   to me

for a shred of sympathy
and could I not help but weep
with him

in his hour of despair
did my heart not stop
for this man

for the poor and wretched
of humanity
didn't I close my eyes

like a hurt child to feel
the boundless passion of inwardness
in every man opened by suffering

but when I opened my eyes
looking for something hopeful
desolation

I waited for some light
I hoped for light
but darkness came over me

and in the pit of my stomach
a cauldron boils
endlessly

days flow into days
like a miserable diarrhea
I wake in the morning

and there's no sun
no ray of friendship
I stand up crying

in the squares
in the bars
in the cafés

and I'm looked at as a brother
to dragons or lizards
crocodiles are my companions

owls and screeching ostriches
are the comrades of my
plaintive shriek of despair

my skin hangs on me
like a tanned wolfhide
my bones melt with fever

my lyre is stretched
to the pitch of wailing
my flute

is a voice turned
to a siren song
in a human holocaust.

CHAPTER 3 1

I came to a decision
behind my eyes
not to let them wander

over the innocent bodies
of young girls
I refocused their attention

what decision am I thus allowed
to see reaching into this world
from behind God's highest cloud

what sense of human
natural rightness
beyond the senses

is it really disaster
for the cold-hearted
hard-core manipulators

of sympathy and affection
devastating twisters
of all feeling in their paths

doesn't he see me
standing openly in the aisle
isn't that his light each step I take follows

if I walked beside high vanity
self-made lights of deception
and let my foot pull me dumbly

into the shadows of bitterness
then let my heart be weighed like stone
on an honest scale

in his hand of justice
and he'll know the lightness
my heart still clings to

if I let my legs
carry me away
in blind animal pride

or let my heart go
to the blood-lust of the world
before my naked eyes

or let my hands indulge themselves
in the mud and gravel of cement
for a wall between us

then let another mouth
eat all
I've worked and sweated for

and all the seeds I've planted
in the ground in my mind in the body
of my wife

be uprooted   totally
if I gave my heart away
          blindly

          to the cold deception
          of a heartless woman
               or the wife

          left innocently alone
          in the sanctuary
          of my neighbor's home

     if I consciously even dreamed
               myself there
     let my wife swallow every drop

          of my lifeblood my honor
               in the seed
          of every passing man

     let them worship between her thighs
     as greedily as men suddenly released
          from death sentences

               then let her rise
          to become their servant
     to wash their sheets while I weep for her

     while my eyes go blank with despair
          before the total explosion
                    of a life

          I'd be guilty of a fire
     swallowing up the air around me
          destroying the spirit of others

as it's magnified in the mirror
of my silent rage within
gone blind with desperation

all my hopes dreams desires
utterly consumed
in the passionate proof

of my lifelong ignorance
boiling up within   temptation
for an untouchable woman

and forgetting that I'm a man
descended from men and women
who held their love humbly

as the free gift
of a baby in their arms
deserving adoration

if I coldly turned away
from the open heart or hand
of my humble servant

anyone I put
consciously or not
in a place to serve me

and who did so   freely or not
then where am I
when I'm in God's presence

how will I come to ask for
what no one can demand
the free gift of love

no longer mine to give
as I turned cold and heartless
in this body he gave me

that he made for us all equally
in the wombs of women
he alone   shaping us there

one creator
one hand moving
one conscious subject

if I refused
the needs of the poor
given to my spirit to bear

if I refused a woman   homeless
having lost her husband
and turned to me

a man in her eyes
growing dim with tears
someone other to look on

for help in the overpowering
needs one life faces
alone for the sake of others

if I swallowed my morsel of food
alone in the face of even one orphan
who had none

if I didn't raise that boy
as his father   that girl
as her true compass

if I've seen someone naked
hopelessly exposed
having lost the shirt off his back

or a poor man woman or saint
who barely ever had one
if that body was not a blessing

I was given to warmly embrace
with fleece from my flocks
if I lorded it

over anyone
because I had the cold advantage
of friends in high places

then let my arm be wrenched
out from its socket
my writing hand fall limp

the pen slip from my fingers
words dry up on my lips
because the turning of God

away from us   as we may turn away
is utter devastation
the dark side of the moon

I couldn't stand there
or breathe
unless he gave me some wisdom

to learn to shield myself
learning by facing terror
that love protects us

if I put my faith in gold
filled my sack of pride
with money

and talked to myself
as if I were precious metal
saying I hold my own security

if I stood up straight
held my head high
encased in rigid armor

the tin shield of fortune
I thought was self-made
forged with my own hand

if I stared into the sun   inwardly
mesmerized or blindly enlightened
struck by its shining riches

if I ever stood hypnotized
before the dreamlike beckoning
of the full moon rising   silver and gold

letting my heart be captured
by cults of sensuality
becoming a slave

to my own enlightenment
handed over to the power
of some physical light or master

some magical dazzling myth
obscuring the light of history on
the pages of human struggling

from generation to generation
to be free of idols and false images
and the hand holding the ax

at whose edge we tremble
dazzled by the glinting beauty
of secret fear or evil

as it slices through our thought
until we can't hold together
can't contain the reality

of opposing forces of energy
the physical struggle inside
of good and evil

if I fell
before idols
separating thought from feeling

if I kissed my own hand
to blow kisses
to some material body in the sky

then that is the height of superstition
the queen of lies
in the face of God

like incest
denying my nature
cutting off my human hand

if I secretly exulted
to learn my enemy
was cut down

struck down by his mean thought
like lightning
where he was hiding

if I let bitterness
slither through my lips
to poison his character

then let the men closest to me
pin me down
devour my flesh with passion

twisting my desire
to share with anyone hungry
my portion of meat

if I left a passing stranger
to sleep in the street
naked to darkness

and didn't open my door
to the open road
sharing my light and warmth

if I have hidden my sins
in a hole
in my heart

like the common herd
covering up the truth
with dirt and litter

because I was afraid to stand out
from the herd   afraid
of common gossip

and contemptuous eyes
of the self-righteous   boring in
with the cold severity of rock-drills

if I stood terrified at that thought
mute
crippled in the heart

afraid to open it or my mouth
to face my own weakness
the petty lies to myself

that I could not even walk
out my door
with my head on frontwards

then I would not deserve the paper
I'm writing on
but here it is!

this is my voice
reaching out for the ear
open to hear it

where is the hearing   the time and place
to make my suffering real
an indictment a list of crimes

even if it were longer than a book
I'd carry it on my shoulders
with honor

I'd wrap it around me like a royal robe
bind it around my head
like a royal turban

I'd walk up to my judge
and lay out my heart like a map
before him

this incredible gift of a heart
feeling
my true thoughts

holding the history book of my life
open to his light
light is my defense!

as confident as a prince
I'd put my life on the line
in the words that are given me

in this court invisible to me
transparent as clean air
before the judge I live to hear

and if my land cried out against me
indicting me with the tears
that ran down in furrows

man made
on the face
of the earth

if I plucked the riches
its fruit   filling my mouth
and gave back nothing

not even a thought
expanding
in gratitude

if I have planted
any cause for anger
in the minds of its tillers

if one migrant worker cried out
because I forced the breath
of integrity out of him

then instead of wheat
let my hand reap
thorns

let it force to no end
this thistle
of a pen

let weeds grow
and cover this page
instead of words that grow wheat

and here for now is ended
the poem
Job speaks.

Ecclesiastes

TRYING TO establish a date for *Ecclesiastes* helps reveal how later Hebrew poets collaborated with earlier ones. The book was written in the third century B.C., working over material dating back to the seventh century B.C., which was based on even older scrolls, perhaps going back to King Solomon's court in the tenth century B.C. Our actual author, however, is the Qohelet who imagined himself King Solomon in the third century B.C.—as leading scholars date it—a time when Greek was becoming the lingua franca in Judea.

The multilayered history is characteristic of the texts of biblical poets, just as it would be of the later, Talmudic writers. A natural irony inheres in the reader's recognition of seemingly "quoted" older material—to reproduce the effect in English requires an emphasis on the psychological dimension. Unless the translator creates a self-critical frame of reference, the old homilies and clichés that Qohelet is intentionally defrocking will come out sounding like the clichés themselves.

Ecclesiastes is a Jewish critique of the pagan genre known as wisdom literature, as well as a more subtle commentary on specifically Jewish conventions of wisdom literature. But the layers of embedded older works allows the poet to compose a moving poem, rather than a detached text. In its ceaseless ebb and flow, its unmasking of clichés and conventional wisdom, the poem depicts the process of awareness itself (as the prophets attempted in their own manner). No philosophy coheres throughout the poem, much less any theology; instead, we are left with a feeling of elation, just as we would be after an effective blues. The poet, wrapped in the trappings of his stubbornly Hebraic culture, finds a way to embrace a difficult world while seemingly rejecting it.

There is a residue of Babylonian cynicism, but it is transformed, along with Greek stoicism, into a Jewish version of earthiness. When the book recommends the benefits of going to a house of mourning over a house of mirth, it is also affirming the Jewish joy in an ethics of doing good works (while lightly bathing the pious sentiment in self-parody). When *Ecclesiastes* was translated into Western languages, it began to sound too much like the worldly material it assimilated and critiqued. Even today, conventional Bible interpreters, particularly non-Jewish ones, mistakenly assume the book is full of corroding doubt.

❧ *Ecclesiastes* ❧

I

You can't take it with you
a breath
all we take in

in a life of action
and exhaustive playback
breath into breath

what progress
what dumb thing can we make
under the sun

out of human hands
greater than our sweat, glistening
in the brief flash of a human life

generations rise and fall
to the earth
that hardly changes

the sun also rises
and falls, gliding
beneath us

back to its starting place
like wind always returning
to us—from any direction

rushing past us
turning and returning
all rivers run

to a body, a sea
that hardly changes
like our deepest thoughts

contained in history
and the seabed of instinct
our words exhaust us

we are speechless
before this flowing
our eyes and ears

forever look and hear
and that's all they know
perfect little machines

everything that happens
happened
happens again

there is nothing new
to grow wild about
under the sun

including the man wildly shouting
"Look, this is new!"
he lived ages ago

in the beginning of time
before records
and even tomorrow

with its memory machines
is lost in space
by the men approaching the end.

11 (1 : 12)

I, the poet
was a king
in Jerusalem

I opened my mind
to explore to feel
everything

every reflection
under the sun:
an overpowering work

God gave a man
to make
with his life

I saw everything happening
under the sun
you can't take it with you

you breathe out
and a little wind shakes the world
alive around you

you can go with the wind
until you're exhausted
or against it and blue-faced

you can't save your breath
and you can't take
what isn't there

a tree bends to the sun
we can't straighten it
our mind can't overpower it

I said in my mind
I've grown rich
on experience

I'm the richest man
in Jerusalem
but what is this mind

and this desire
to abandon ourselves
in front of it

and I almost went mad
trying to add up
what I had

I grew nervous
I couldn't think straight
I was lost in the sun . . .

it's painful to hold
everything you own
inside

we can't take it—
rooted
to the air.

III (2 : 1)

I said in my mind
I will abandon myself
take life as it comes

but that is another mirage
the laugh is on the escapee
as life passes him by

I made this experiment
drink and smoke a lot
embrace pleasure

but meanwhile: keep my purpose clear
and open to insight
think: what's best

for a brief little life,
thinking or feeling?
so I set to work

in the grand style
building an _oeuvre_
ten books in five years

works of love and despair
naked and shameless
I was married and divorced

I went to all the parties
the glittering eyes
and wit: passion-starved

a trail of blinding jewels
of experience behind me
more than any king in Jerusalem

I tried on every life-style
I pushed to the center
through many gaudy affairs

I was surrounded by stars
singers and dancers
and fresh young bodies

to choose among
at the slightest whim
I was high and I was courted

but I kept my sense of purpose
every imaginable distraction
surrounded me

I opened myself to sheer
luxury of feeling
my mind was out there

on the windy ledge
and this is what I learned:
we can take in *anything*

and we are still empty
on the shore of the life
our blood flows to.

IV (2 : 13)

Then I looked up
above my personal horizon
to see the sky

outstretching the sea
as wisdom
lightens a heavy body

a wise man's eyes
are in his head
while the absentminded

professor or egoist
disdains to wipe his glasses
while he sinks to the bottom of the sea

but wisdom as quickly evaporates
the moment a body dies
shipwrecked beneath its headstone

the most penetrating realist
hits rock bottom
six feet under

and the farthest seer
on the beachhead of life
gets his mouthful of sand

so even wisdom is a pocket
turned inside out
when it's time to pay the body's burden

the blind will lead the wise
beyond the furthest suburb of memory
into total obscurity

reentering the city of the future
as dust to be swept away
from the pages of the present

so where will I go
with this wisdom   this breath
in the sail of a fool

and so I turned again
blind as a hurricane
against the sea of life

where all works sink
like jettisoned cargo
under the lidless eyeball of the sun

the whole cargo of civilization
was a weight on my shoulders
my life's work dead weight

all life depressingly empty
hollow as cardboard dumbbells
in a bad circus

a bad dream
in which my fame honor wealth
all the earnings disappeared in a thought

in a dream circus where a clown waited
cocky in his painted face
of identity

to inherit all my works
and I am not to know
if there's a mind and heart of depth

beneath the greasepaint
or it really is the face
of life's unrelenting sideshow

in which my successor my reader
discounts my lifework
in a snobbish indifference

to the working man   common or
artist (and helmsman
of the direction life has dealt him

in working his will over it)
and my books my record
fade and crack in the sun

cast overboard like ballast
all that I've learned not even a shadow
cast in the desert

a little shade for integrity
my wealth empty as a mirage
of water

and so my heart sank
to the bottom
in the dry well of despair

empty of illusions
about the fine sweat we produce
under the sun

slave to a desire
for *whose* "one fine day"?
each day another sigh

accumulated
another groan for the harvest
of rich disappointment

each night
our hearts lie wide awake
lashed to the body's ship

ferrying that load of heartache
from day to day
with the constant of breathing

to fill the sail
and ripple the pages
of an empty book

the best thing for a man
is to eat drink and be
just be

satisfaction in the flow
of works and days
as it is all the work

of a creator
making me
aware of my body

and by its satisfaction
my need to be here
a pen in the hand of the Lord—

who will feel the pressure
of his will
if not I?

and if what I do is pleasing
in his eyes
I will see through my own

a work graced with beauty
a world open
to a fresh page of understanding

on which I create
my own happiness
an articulate self-knowledge

and if I project
only my own vision
with my tiny primitive hand-driven will

I will be the ancestral hunter
and gatherer   a slave
to the stalking of wealth and power

and the snobbish mask of nobility
the illusion of living
(in ignorance) forever

which at my death will be handed over
to another man   an open one
deep enough to hold his fortune within

fulfilling his creator
in the reality of commerce
between vision and self-awareness

adding a living dimension
to the flat mirror
of the future

the mirror in which puffed-up
self-centered lords
are drowning in vanity.

v (3 : 1)

There is time for everything to happen
under the sun   to lift anchor
in the flow of seasons

everything has its moment
under the uncounted stars
its season of desire

summer of being born
winter of dying
spring of seeding

fall of reaping
winter of killing
summer of healing

spring of uprooting
fall of rebuilding
fall of weeping

spring of laughing
winter of lamenting
summer of dancing

summer making love
winter of surviving
spring of embracing

fall of parting
spring of finding
fall of losing

winter keeping
summer discarding
summer of hot tears

winter of consoling
winter of silence
summer speaking out

spring in love
fall in anger
winter of war

and hating
summer of peace
and hugging

but what can a man add
to the interworking of things
of his own intrinsic value

is a man anything different
whether or not the sweat and thought
is wrung from his body like a rag

I have thought about the tatters
and felt the finest mindspun silk
these are clothes created for us

all men and women wear them
the work of their creator
who has dressed everything in space

each event in time
tailored to its place
and he puts a mannequin of desire

before the hearts and minds of men
so that we long to dress ourselves
create a vision of the future

in which our lives fit today
with a similar beauty of rightness
but the longing for a world of our own

defeats us   the world defeats us
like a mirror we may not look behind
though a taste of creation propels us forward

I have seen as with a long look
the best a man can make
is to create his own goodness

out of a clear image of himself
the satisfaction in simply being alive
the pleasure of his own eyes

seeing
as long as he can
as long as he lives

just to eat and drink
the fruits of your work
is a gift from your creator

the world is a gift that lasts
he gave
and nothing more can be added

no matter can be erased
the universe beyond us
came before us

and the wonder of our presence
is that we feel it all
in the awe before our own little creations

in the awe of our hearts moving
closer to their creator
as we ourselves become stiller

the grace to be still
in the flow of all creation
for a moment

and through the window of a moment
the opening of eyes within eyes
to see the ancient perspective of time

painted in a landscape with light
the future the eyelids opening
as of a prehistoric creature

under the ungraspable sky
that was
is

and will be: the airless height
of understanding   pure space we pursue
like fish the worms of conscience

and are drawn to
like a seed to air
in a new baby's wail

like a man to a woman
like a creature
to his maker

V I (3 : 1 6)

But when I looked further
under the sun I found
sitting in the seat of justice

beasts
and in the lap of wisdom
lizards

I heard myself thinking
the creator has made a road
from the heights of wisdom

to the conscience in every man
and each must find his way
meanwhile the court is abandoned

to the claws of influence
the school is abandoned
to the gnawing animal of despair

a season of disbelief
blows sand in the eyes
of the Lord's creatures

and I saw clearly
men are not higher than the camels
they must ride on

horse and rider
both arrive together
at the end of the journey

their skeletons come clear
like maps to nowhere
buried underground

their bones gallop into dust
together   they both run out
of breath

a breath is all
a creature takes in
in a lifetime of action

it joins the infinite grains of sand
on the shore of the life
its blood flowed to

who knows if the man's spirit
rises
while his faithful steed's falls

who has seen this parting of ways
in the midst of his own journey
fixed in life's precious saddle

and so I came to see
man is made to be happy
taking care and keeping clear

his own vision
embracing the world
with the arms of his work

along the road
of his conscience
who or what

manner of creature or act
could bring him far enough
out of himself

out of the sun's pull
to see the unbreathing future
beyond the living present

and beyond the little picture show
of stars and galaxies
cheapened by superstition.

V I I (4 : 1)

Then I returned
to consider again
the oppression constant as daylight

returning under the sun
here are the cisterns of tears
of all men oppressed

by the ravenous animal
of injustice   no one human
enough to offer an arm

and shoulder of consolation
here are the fists of power
in sleeves of comforting armor

the dead are better off
having found some consolation
more than the living

still trembling inside
before a concealed weapon
death

and better off than all
the unborn   uncalled
to being witness

to the heavy work
of men holding down
men

drowning each other in air
absorbing the power and
dimming the light

in the bloodstream
under a sky
made of skin

human energy I noted again
comes from a heart's
envy of the world

it sees itself in mind's mirror
as a galley slave   its horror
gives birth to "free" enterprise

so, concealed beneath the surface of excellence
and talent and plain hard work
is a motor of fear

running against each man's neighbor
and the fuel
is suppressed desire

pressure to be free of the power
of others   and so
breathing itself becomes a mechanism

empty of spirit
men are busily at work
building models of this

the race is on
to the heart
of the human machine

and men are proud of this ladder of "progress"
of where they stand
in the eyes of status (their neighbor)

then there is the man who is
his own totem:
a brain made out of wood

hands glued together with indifference
to the rat race
thinned by idiocy instead of tension

so which do you prefer
a vain idiot or an idiot vanity
how about a breath of fresh air

instead of rigorous incense!
a handful of quietness
instead of both hands shaking at the grind wheel

and the heavy perfumes of oil and sweat . . .
then I looked away and saw more
futility masquerading under the sun

the man or woman determined to be alone
no one beside them
no family no children

so why are they working so hard
salting away money and power
piling up credit promiscuously

around the clock
no time to even think
just who am I sacrificing

my time my pleasure for
who am I and who will know me
when I'm gone

the apple of this one's eye
is gilded to conceal
a core of depression

but just as oppressive the clichés
like two heads are better than one
sure: they cover each other's failings

if one of them falls
the other can lift him up
yes there's brilliant logic in this!

for how foolish one looks when he sprawls
having fallen all alone
without the grace of even someone's worried look!

also two who are sleeping together
get some warmth on cold nights
one alone gets only cold   and looks ridiculous

and is exposed to attack
while two link together
and with another make a chain   to brandish

or a coat of mail
yes friend- and kinship
is a power that binds

like word to word an oath (however false)
to keep or hurl with confidence—
but one all alone is blown in the wind.

V I I I (4 : 13)

They say it's better to be poor
when young—and wise
than a rich, old celebrity

a king   clamped
in the throne of his mind
unable to hear the clamoring streets . . .

the youth can walk freely
out of a king's prison
to become a king himself

while the born leader
even become a dictator
can only topple over

in his heavy mental armor
reduced to his knees
like a wordless beggar

but then I thought about that youth
rising to take his place
how the mass of people were inspired

by him   by his success
as people embrace the rags-
to-riches morality play

the longing masses
eager to start over
to wipe the messy history slate clean

and suddenly the man as all men
is gone   and his son
slouches in his place

rain has fallen on the history books
and the sun bleached it dry
for the new generations

which are endless in number
as were the ones preceding him
and for both alike he is unknown

the living page of his time
bled white out of memory
another page lost in the sea of the present

where even the beautiful craft
of inspired imagination
have their sails reduced to tatters

and their vain hopes discolored
like old photos
by the vague tears of sentiment

the memory of that star
like any moment of triumph or despair
is cut loose from the mooring of its time

adrift like a lifeless raft
after an explosion
after the countless explosions of moments

and the photos a living mind has made
in fits of hope or doubt
forgotten utterly as the sounds

of shutters clicking open
spoken words
a wind has blown away.

I X (4 : 1 7)

Watch your step
when your feet automatically carry you
unconsciously   to the temple

it's better to see yourself
and feel
what you are doing

than offer blind obedience
but go in
with your eyes open

and keep your heart open
to the right way
don't lead your heart blindly

into a marriage of convenience
don't be a fool   except for love
of the truth

and then you will know
what you love
and if you must suffer it

the pain will have some value
you'll know how to carry that weight
inside   your arms still open

to hold the life
you are given
as your own

those who watch their hearts
before they take a step
walk into sleeves of darkness

their hearts comfortably dressed
for the time they sacrifice to religion
walking down that narrow aisle

so richly upholstered   a tunnel
sealed against the life flowing
from the real temple's spirit

it is too dimly lit there
for them to know
what good or evil they are married to.

Ecclesiastes

X (5 : 1)

But don't open your mouth
too quickly or spill out your heart
in an alphabet soup of prayers

his vision spreads across heaven
where a mouthful of words aren't needed
and you are on earth

where words can come cheaply
to someone so low to the ground
he can't foresee the next minute

the next second when suddenly
his mood changes
and he is denying what he just said

bad dreams daydreams fantasies
spread like blinding steam
from too much living in the moment

too many things to do
with no pause for real reflection
and hot air streams from the mouth

of someone who talks too much
if you've promised to do something
if you've sworn to God

do it
he has less time than you have
to sit in the steambath

and wish the world away
pay what you owe even as it pains
and your eyes will clear a path for you

better yet don't make promises
you can't keep
especially to yourself: it's your mouth

in your body
so don't let it betray
flesh of your flesh

and when you do
and when the messenger comes to collect on it
take your foot out of your mouth

don't pretend it was perfectly natural
to mistakenly be licking someone's foot
don't pretend your mouth is not in your head

but respect the work of your creator
who put it there   he is perfectly right
to be angry with your swollen voice

and to puncture the blister of things
you've accumulated around you
with the grasping hands

he also presented to you
along with the gift of language
you infect with mouths of stale air

from the disembodied chatter
of fantasies and dreams
false gods and persons

streaming from the unchecked mind
inflating the world with unreal messages—
wake up   and trust your maker.

X I (5 : 1 0)

A lover led by silver
will never embrace enough of her
his arms won't even reach behind her

and one in love with more
than he can hold
gets only more of the same: frustration

and another vain kiss the wind
blows away
like seed not firmly planted

in a body of earth
a measure equal
to a body's need

the more food the land produces
the more people grow up
to eat it

what satisfaction is this easy multiplication
to the stomach of its owner
who grows fat in the eyes

feasting on his own desire
to be bright and superior
in the social mirror

of shallow eyes
a surface flattened for respect
adding up to a fat reflection

while the undistracted worker
tired from sheer indivisible labor
melts into sleep

like a cube of sugar
in a glass of tea
regardless of what he's eaten

but the man bloated with possessions
living in a dream-stomach of selfhood
a pig of identity

this man digesting property
indiscriminately as a camel
in the garbage dumps on the outskirts

of Beersheba
this rich man with a full stomach
inside and outside

gulping the wine of self-imagery
and still this man just can't fall asleep
his peace sits at the bottom of his glass

a lump of stone
and the man who hides his wealth
like the man who lives alone

grows sick on the stale breath of himself
ends up in a daydream
where he tosses away his fortune

in an impulsive fit
and the hoard of his ego
falls to pieces within him

nothing to pass on
to his son   the milk soured in the heat
of a sudden passionate thought

his hand empty
the glass shattered on the floor
rock bottom   the pit

naked and wet
as when he came through
the womb where he was fashioned

and he will follow his mother
back again to a deeper
source in earth

the mother of us all
stripped to the dry skeleton
barest image of a human

falling back
into the hidden hand
of creation

his own hands slowly unforming
and all that they held
all the land and fruits

of labor   gone
another daydream gone sour
another life led down the path

into a falling darkness
another illusion for the instincts
naked he came naked returns

alone with his reality
a life struggling to grasp
something in the wind

to make something more
of his own breath
than the spirit his efforts obscure

the labor that eats away inside
like another hungry worker
toiling away in the darkness inside

this companion worker this utter
reality   born in frustration
in a fertile mind   bred in worry and anger

and this is what I learned
what's worth struggling to learn
is as beautiful as being

working to eat drink and be
satisfied in the flow
of works and days

like water shining under the sun
harnessed
to the energy burning within

the little sun of a lifetime
God has given   so
let's have a good time

in the simple space and time
of human vision
that I may hold

in my hands
like a telescope
the fact of memory

embracing the world
with the feeling of real arms
warm from their labor

and to those of us allowed
luxury and property and
grace to enjoy them

in this gift of a body
happy in the sun
on a smooth shore of a life

content by the glistening sea
of our own fine sweat
which brought us to a home we feel good in—

that home is a vessel
a gift of God
in which we travel awhile

a little journey equal to the breadth
of our vision
the depth of our memory

a present to us
buoyant on the waves
connecting past and future

the surges of wind and breath
keeping a mind clear
through dark passages of fear

that life is passing us by
blood washing over stone
making us rigid with fear   stone

but God makes a clearing in the heart
we gather our thoughts there   a labor
mirroring the work that reveals us to ourselves.

XII (6 : 1)

Another thing I see
weighing men down
in the invisible backpack

harnessed to every walker in the sun
or at the feet of one freely standing
is the load of injustice

a man or woman shining
in the eyes of their community
standing tall in mirrors of themselves

sure of their identity in the stylish dress
of God-given talents
confident on red carpets of success

rolled out from houses that hold
everything you could wish for
a happy family and nothing to wish for

a spirit filled to the brim
a table spread before him
but then—he can't eat:

he hasn't been allowed an heir
a visible future
as the present eats away inside him

someone else embodies his desire
his appetite materializes as another man
real or imagined

his fortune feeds that person
a stranger in the lap
of his reality

he stands before an empty mirror
staring into the abyss of vanity
unforeseen

(some other man will absently lounge
in the warmth and care
he skilled his hands to open)

and even if he were surrounded
with a hundred sons and daughters
and lived to a ripe old age

happiness could elude him a hundred ways
like echoes bouncing off stone
in a desert canyon

echoes from one unguarded shriek of recognition
terror-flash of the material world
black glimpse of an eternity

a nightmare instead of a miracle
a nuclear bomb
instead of a warming sun

all in a moment stripped bare by frustration
his soul stripped like a woman
in the midst of a crowded market that

was the world of his possessions
even if he were to live forever
that moment would gape behind him

like a freshly dug grave
the echo of violent recognition
and the vast explosive mirror-reality

of antimatter   blind to his reflection
in a soul   irreducible
shaping the universe within   heaven and earth

but he can only see the face of horror
the hot flash of recognition: only the material evidence
a momentary picture but haunting him everywhere

a stillborn child   even a fetus
aborted is better off
than someone in the midst of everything

life has to offer and still restless
in the desert of awareness   blunt exposure
to a sense of happiness somewhere lost

like the innocent whiteness of skin
under a desperate tan
worse off than that embryo of darkness

innocent of the self-made light
of inner desperation   who comes
in passionate night sighs

and leaves before dawn
no one seeing its face
its name its sex bundled in darkness

better off not having breathed
or seeing its image inflated
in its own eyes

for it never had to bitterly wish
for a comforting darkness
to be gratified in

even if the man lived a thousand years
two thousand
what good is the sum of his breaths of air

if he's satisfied with nothing but a wish
with which to pay for his journey
to the same dust as all that have beginnings

this person's work kept his mouth full
and still he gasps for air
on the shore

what difference does it make
if it's Siberia or the Riviera
to a fish out of water

what good will books and travel
do us   wise man and fool
flop in the net of their longing

following the wind
our breath longs to catch
as if we could be somewhere else

and the realist making his way
in caution and poverty
thinks he should have been born rich

this makes bitterness "real" instead of "imagined"?
it's better to hold a bull by the horns
than have two in the bush?

what you see is what you get:
more bull   the eyes never stop
walking down that narrow aisle

of the universal supermarket
which is another illusion
like theories of objectivity

like the posters of mild Hawaii
we make what we see
with the eyes of a double

longing to be merely here
in our shoes
learning how to speak walk and be

more than a spectator
with the watery baby-eyes of an old man
just to be somebody somewhere anywhere: fully alive

this too is deadly illusion
just wanting to be
where we are already

pursuing the wind
that blows through us
as if we could be another.

X I I I (6 : 1 0)

Anything that has a beginning
everything
was a seed in the pot

planted before existence
and named by men
as it flowed into the world

man is also a kind of flower
whose growth is defined
and all that flows from his hands

and with our own little names
we can't argue with our creator
a name that's boundless

beyond identity
like death which takes back our names
and gives them to the living

the more words we use
the more bricks for the mausoleum
building castles in the air

that are ancient relics
the moment we exhale
passed on to ignorant children

when we die
they prefer sand castles
and when the tide comes in they will not cry

but watch   fascinated
no better or worse
than all preceding men

who knows
what the right thing to do is
with a life

that walks across a stage
of air
in a bathing costume of flesh

until night falls like a gown
over a beautiful woman
who sleeps alone

only our shadows remain
impotent watchmen
on the shore of the life

our blood flowed to
and suddenly they too are gone
as the sun again rises

piercing all wishes and dreams
and romances of the future
with the bones of light

we are stripped awake   leaving
a shadow on the shore
that had not seen its own body.

X I V (7 : 1)

They say it's better to keep your name clean
than your body   whether bathing
in baby oil holy oil or covering a stink

with expensive deodorant
no man stinks more than a dead man
but, if left behind is the inner perfume

of a good name—then his deathday is happy
so no more false happy birthdays
until a man is dead

then he can be famous
without having to grease a palm or wear
the painted mask of success . . .

they say it's better to be with a family
burying their dead
than one celebrating successful occasions

for all will pass beyond
these forgotten fêtes
your vision will serve to remind them

you aren't eating your heart away
in feasts of gratitude or envy
but opening it

to the face of loss
all must wear
and all will remember your presence

they say the face of grief
is better than the laughing
party masks of plastic

the raw skin of sadness
though bad for one's complexion
reddens the blood strengthens the heart

and improves the mind
a wise heart is anchored
in a natural seriousness   at home

even at death with its wall of silence
even in a house that wails
in tune with hearts exposed and beating

while, running away from itself
a foolish heart capsizes
in a sea of nervous giggles

and flails desperately
behind a happy face of plastic
swimming back to its place at the party

under a paper moon
calmed by the stereo dutifully playing
"it's only a paper moon"

they say better listen to stinging
criticism from someone knowing
what they're talking about

Ecclesiastes

than lending your ear to "friends"
you turn on like a radio
to the muzak of approval

the best tunes become idiotic
when translated for the mouse-eared
masses   inertia

is playing even more softly
under a muzak of desire
to be somewhere else

to escape into a soft sculpture
of the world created
and played on by heavies

having no idea what to do
with themselves   an empty talent
bottling air   milking respect

from wide-eyed calves looking
vainly for approval: the hot breath
in the nostrils of a bull

is what you get if not despair
served in silver trophy cups
empty as the occasions they honor

but even humility in the wisest person
allowing him to say
exactly what he sees

resisting influence and flattery
hardens into a statue of identity
to grace the social scene

"words to the wise" spoken at a café
like the coffee itself turns to oil
greasing the social mechanism

and he is also a helpless victim
of naïve hearts and eyes
he impresses his image upon

in his own naïve sexuality
mistaking love for innocence
gratitude for understanding

they say it's better to listen
to what you think
you have to say   inner ear

and eye open to what happens
to the event
in speaking in becoming a mirror a judge

everyone is hungry for images
of themselves   better see through that
than start up new fantasies

keep your conscience a clear window
to see through
as your death approaches from a distance

better a happy deathday
unsurpassed
than happy birthdays increasingly desperate

let what's there be
to feel smell hear see
before you gulp down something

like a hungry dog or baby
better to see a thing come clear
in the emulsion of time

than lose your integrity
in the rush of pride
to impose an image on the movie

to expose a frame too quickly
outside the nature time
of creation

don't get mad and impatient
restrain yourself
when everyone seems to be getting ahead

it's a stampede of mice
a rat race   madness
quickening the mass of Disney hearts

don't look back in anger
at boats you think you missed
or whine about good old days

while you frown in the idiot's mirror
reading wrinkles as ancient ciphers of a dilemma
central to the origin of the big cartoon

in the past most people are living in
the vast expanding bubble of "progress"
that suddenly bursts

throwing water in the face
of the philosopher on the beach
dreaming of fountains of youth

what depths of disappointment spring
from fantastic wells of expectation
sunk in the false bottom of fantasy land

don't be so dumb as even to inquire
in the studied falsetto of a scholar
where has the past gone?

it will smack you in the face
for having turned your head
at every passing fancy

of knowledge shaped by the girdle of progress
then there are those who study it
accumulating knowledge as if it were money

better to marry it
better yet inherit it
so there's time to sit in the shade

after gazing into the sun
its reflection off the metal
of coin

to sit in the cool shadow
of the mind's reflection   safe
in the reality of sun

the difference is
(between accumulating and having)
the wise man has a life within

a harbor for his ship to come in
illuminated by an inner reality
feeling the sun's power as light

falling around a field or page
not to possess it from towers
but letting it be revealed

observe this working of God
light   in its own time
as it reveals the touch of its creator

a tree bends to the sun
we can't straighten it
our mind can't overpower it

when a good day
comes your way
embrace it

and when the bad one arrives   watch out
but patience   observe the contrast
light creates a room for shadow

one creator made each day
so we don't build up expectation
as a wall

but may see the stones fall
names and reputations
material ripped away to an open view

of the present around us
the dimension of depth
sweeping between light and shadow

between inside and outside
the dynamic of waves
sweeping away the tower

climbed by the one thinking he was master
of what he could survey: past and future
but it is drowned

along with elaborate constructions of myth
fortune-telling and other dark fortresses
built for a false security

each day is constructed anew
in the flow of time   perfect as the sea
bearing a ship to its destiny

that is _felt_ to be there
and in that feeling we can find no fault
with the nights and days that surprise us

in our beds of doubt or certainty
we are made perfectly awake
to the fathomless depth of creation.

X V (7 : 1 5)

I've seen everything
in the rich days I've walked through
like a long hall

in a home I thought I owned
and from life's windows
I've seen it all

though inside I had nothing
but a little wind
to keep my eyes from closing

I saw those who breathe deeply
in the rare atmosphere
of righteousness

and I saw them dying in it
from lack of oxygen
while cynics whose mouths are full

of lies grow strong and healthy
and live long lives
in their sewers of deceit

so don't climb up high
after perfection
don't get carried away

in the altitude of lucidity
nobody remembers who you are
when you fall on your face identityless

like a bright leaf blown by a wind
as strong and true
as a will driven beyond the imperfect body

but don't bend to natural forces
too easily   don't hold on
to the rail when the ship is sinking

don't cling to yourself like a child
to its toy
don't be a baby

still wailing inwardly
for attention   ruthless
don't stoop so low

to wear the wound of need on your arm
to play on the innocence of others
to be selfish as stone inside

the idol of yourself
why swallow a stone
the stone of bitterness you cast

and die before you've opened
a door to human kindness—
locked in the arms of deceit

squeezing the life away
of you and your victims   don't suffocate
don't be too self-involved

or selfless—hold on
but keep your mind open
let God anchor your conscience

freeing you to be
neither ego's slave nor wisdom's fool
you swim beyond the wreck

of single-minded arrogance
first one arm then the other
and a sense of a higher, deeper order . . .

on the one hand intelligence
is a stronger defense than
a pantheon of pious figureheads

there isn't a righteous cause on earth
without its empty-headed champions
promoting their own hot air

not one perfect man or woman
who is always right   uncompromised
by the slightest distortion in the mirror

by which he knows himself
and forgets himself too: the flaw
in taking memory for granted

a distorting memory   reflected
through the glass of
a highly compressed fear

for it will explode as sure as a star
just as the present is always erupting
dispersing the precious crockery of the past

into the lap of dozing Justice
who has forgotten this appointment
with the bill collector of Time. . . .

The Inner Call

ISAIAH

JEREMIAH

ZECHARIAH

JONAH

Isaiah

THE FACT that the scope of *Isaiah* is beyond any one poet drew me to consider the core of vision holding the book together. Several poets, writing centuries apart, shared a unique sensibility. Scholarship calls this sensibility "the school of Isaiah," allowing for many other poets whose work has been lost or who acted largely as curators and restorers of an earlier Isaiah's text. For example, the autobiographical section that begins Chapter 6 was clearly not written by the poet who set down his autobiographical experience at the beginning of Chapter 40.

Taken together, the chapters in *Isaiah* do not progress narratively but present a serial building up of passion and vision, an intuitive architecture of feeling. I've tried to knit together a representation of at least three of the school of Isaiah poets. The feeling for consciousness is fundamental, as it struggles to free itself from conventional myths. To restore a sense of the original poetry's spokenness and withering irony, I attempted to turn modern poetic tradition inside out, playing the grandiose (or prophetic) "I" against the intimacy of a conversational voice. In a similar manner, the first Isaiah lent his oracular voice to the Isaiah poets who came after.

In a central metaphor for prophecy, Isaiah represents self-knowledge as a light to others: the visionary power hidden in every man and woman, beginning with the most oppressed. *Isaiah* becomes a testament to self-consciousness, illustrating how language itself—the quality of *listening* to it—bonds poet to creator.

The poets of the school of Isaiah extend five hundred years after the original prophet in the eighth century B.C. Consider how our religious institutions today prefer their religion in more manageable prose forms. In the same way, the religious establishment during some ancient periods tried to limit poets to the realms of prayer and wisdom literature. Facing this opposition, the poets of the prophetic schools sharpened their poetry further.

The depth of poetry puzzles many readers, who still turn to prose exegesis. But take away the sound, metaphors, and images of Isaiah and we're left merely with a mummified corpse of its meaning. Or worse, we're in the hands of interpreters who take the prophetic metaphors too literally. Parts of Isaiah have been characterized as primitive for their "elaborate ferocity," for instance. Yet, as the critic C. C. Torrey wrote in *The Second Isaiah,* "The prophet was not bloodthirsty, he was only a poet."

There is a broad emotional range to the Isaiah poets, from the fierce satire of Chapter 14 to the tender consolation of Chapter 40. A desire to transform loss into creative vision prevails. "We've papered over loss," from Chapter 52, is typical of an Isaiah poet's refusal to leave it alone. The poets writing in Isaiah's spirit project this self-awareness into the world: "we wandered away/ lost in ourselves// we were all nations/ servants of our own/ interests . . ."

The passion is devoutly self-critical. Opening to pain, to an identity with the lowest, the poorest, the most powerless individual, the poets and prophet become one in recognizing the imaginative freedom this openness allows. For poets, the freedom yields timeless metaphors: "all flesh is grass/ and the reality of love is there/ wild flowers in the field . . ."

❧ *Isaiah* ❧

CHAPTER 1

Listen universe
and ear of earth   turn
to words of your creator

they are witnesses   tuned
to the source of memory
invisible to all that changes:

I brought up children
held them in my presence
and they turn from me

deaf and blind
when even the dumb ox knows
who holds his food

an ass
the trough
its master fills

but Israel knows nothing
of its root in me
sees nothing of where

they come from
who brought them up
nobody knew them helpless and wide-eyed

and they can't stop to remember
to think or to hear themselves thinking
lost in themselves

mindless people
so heavy with repressed guilt
they think they walk lightly when they crawl

fathers in masks of self-pity
sons in poses of self-righteous
pettiness

their backs to creation
they pushed it out of mind
and turned

condemned it as blindly as a slum
they grew up in
they see their true home as a slum

and they refuse to see it
looking through mirror glasses
walking through a false landscape

of their own making   through the rubble
of their distorted image of themselves
grossly attenuated

running away as they run out of time
from the father of their spirit
from the saving dimension of depth

and history reaching back   memory
unfolding space and time
beyond them   beyond change

what part of this people's body
isn't bruised yet
from turning away

still lusting for internal bruises
in the claws of a soulless world
a head naked to despair

a heart exposed to desperation
from bottoms of the feet
to head crown

not a spot on your body
untouched
by the painted hand of vengeance

the revenge of men
painting themselves
with raw animal pride

raw canvas bejeweled
with open wounds and blisters
open to infection

no clean hand to unroll the bandage
no tender selfless arms
to cleanse your spirit

a country totally desolate
cities of ash heaps
fields of mud

trampled by strangers
hordes of them streaming by
leaving you a bystander

in your own land
on desolation row
the daughter of Zion

dear Jerusalem left standing alone
scarecrow
a shed in a cucumber field

a shack in the sea of a vineyard
a ghetto a slum holding on
as if by its teeth

a remnant of survivors
and if the Lord of creation turned his back on us
we'd only be a painful memory   *no* memory!

a tombstone overturned face down
Sodom and Gomorrah
the dark side of the moon

listen to the words
of your creator
blind leaders of Sodom

tune your ears
to the witness of the universe
deaf people of Gomorrah

look up from the self-indulgence
of gilt-edged prayers
the sentimental eyewash

of the time you "sacrifice"
the money of your ritual donations
to make yourself feel better

this is your witness speaking
I've seen enough
of your distracted meditation and mysteries

measured in time and money
heard enough of your sheepish sighs
for a pastoral future

swallowed enough of your toasts
to institutions of repression
smelled enough of your smokestacks

felt enough bodies fall
to their knees
in bloodless words

of posed "uplift"
before monumental paperweights
pious backdrops for photographs

who asked you for pictures
of righteousness
when you come to look for me

trampling through my sanctuary
my library of unwritten
prayer from the heart

with your precious albums
your unreal books
your desperate fantasy of prayer

I want no more sacred mirrors
of yourselves
the microphones of your empty voices

praying for an answer
a travesty of sympathy
like a tape-recorded answer would be

you are so locked in yourselves
your coming out to worship
to readings of my books

becomes the ghost of true spirit
superstitions
of new moons and sabbaths

I can't stand your weird impersonations
of spiritual beings
your minutes of meditation

and Sundays off
I hate that cheap
indulgence of spirit

heavier than lead
I can't bear it
it crushes spirit

I hide from you in light
when you close your eyes
to look for me

when you bow your heads
your prayers will fall
to the floor

your ears are filled with blood
of your own hearts pounding
I won't listen to that desperation

your hands are full of blood
you turn to me
with the blood memory of your slaughtered conscience

wash yourselves
clean your desperate wish
to be loved   clinging

like cheap perfume to your soul
remove your cloaks of status
your veils of sincerity

beneath them you grope for me
like blind animals
laying hands on your brothers and sisters

climbing over them desperately
to appear self-satisfied
before the mirror

before the community of lies
but there in the bed of your hands
your evil lies

there are no roofs over you
in my sight
let me not see it

stop the oppression
learn to see it
respond openly

ask questions
love can answer
what are those beggars on your streets

those window shoppers
those like you depressed
too desperate to even know it

look at them and give
your attention
place your hope in their hands

for they are fatherless and motherless
widows and widowers
totally alone

make them your cause
reach for them
cause them to see you are human

let us come together again
openly
says your creator

though the hands of your desire
are scarlet
they will be clean as sunshine

falling effortlessly
over the city
light as snow light as fleece of lamb

if you are listening
the world will be open
to you

if you hide your heart
you will be slaughtered like cattle
by the hands of desperation

the mouth
of my creator
has spoken

How the beautiful daughter my city
clean light falling around her
has become a whore

she opened the door for love
and light came into her
and shone in her eyes

now you murderers stand naked
in her windows
your house smeared with gaudy paint

of status and power
cheap façades
all sense of proportion lost

in the violent rush for metal
the clasping of silver
to your breasts

the vintage of your heart
love pressed deep in your blood
has become cheap wine

the cream of your people
has mixed with the blood of thieves
in the dark

your leaders are like terrorists
of spirit
spilling your lifeblood

everyone loves to steal
and turn the pages of my books
into worthless money

they hide their loneliness away
in dark asylums
and turn away from orphans

turn away from the naked heart
open to me   exposed by loss
my widows and orphans

leaders lost in the cheap reflection
their metal armor casts
armor they dress their image in

to be princes for whores
lose themselves in silence
in beds of cheap clichés

and so my creator speaks
to those who've repressed him
who oppress each other

Oh I'm tired of defenses
I'm going to lean on
the world's tinsel fences

and crush them
the burden of guilt will fall
on you

with the weight of silence
I will open your hands
as if to cover your eyes from light

and the paper in your fists
will fall
the armor thin as paper

money and contracts: symbols
of the memory loss
that is repressed

instead I'll forgive
with the pure fire of feeling
remembered

you'll share the weight
of each other   with care
the burden of vision

will take form again
in words
as in the beginning

of our speaking   our book
our text of light
it will be *remembered*

with care
in order
to forgive

to forget   to need
to create again
a nation

you will come home
to see yourselves as you are
children of light

to say it in what you do
city of light city of song
city of arms that are strong

that are men and women open inside
embracing
my daughter Jerusalem

Zion will be called
an open ear will be its calling
a light in the window

of the home you can
go back to
the memory whole again

in those that are moving
moved to return
lifted on wings of care

exposed to light
committed to the page
connecting past and future

infinite page of the sky
recording this journey
present journey

from and to
desire
all your children

turning the pages
for others
disarming the blind demands

of domineering pride
the brutal suppression of daylight
for the darkness of a self-centered womb

denying the wonder of the journey
those dictators of hot air
those mindless followers

they are lost together
their memory wiped clean
they will keep nothing

of the precious stones they cling to and defend
they will return to the earth
pried loose from their pebbles

as they left their children straying
from the rock of our desire
the light of our creation

to them it's a violent explosion
they repress
secure in the general darkness

for them a violent uprooting
who put their faith in nature
and their own imitations

industrial idols   cheap paradises
blind to the light
that nourishes all

it will strip them bare
to face their wounded pride
openly

in terror
at the violence of the energy
that was repressed

for a taste of seedless fruit
a sexual knowledge
sucking light's power in

a garden of one's own making
a dream of being seduced
by pride

a dream that will fade
like leaves on dying trees
in a desert oasis

your life will dry up
of unquenchable thirst
for it is really a mirage

no water will bring that dream
to life
you are lost in that desert

the power in your hands
holds a paper doll
for the fire in your mind

your world is a map of paper
you wrap yourself in
and burn

both you and your dream world
burning up together
no one to quench the fire.

CHAPTER 2

These are the words
Isaiah found
before his eyes.

One day
far away from now
distant as the days of creation

the mountain of spirit
in which Israel found
the House of God

that mountain will be revealed
higher
than any earthly mountain

and all nations of the earth
will see it clearly
their hearts go out to it

flowing streams
cleared of fallen wood
moved to come closer

"Let's go up
this mountain of vision
to the House of Israel's God

to learn his ways
to walk
in his ways

to carry his words
books of the Bible
out of Jerusalem"

the words Israel found
before them
in Zion

then the spirit behind them
God
will come forward

to settle the conflicts between us
finally   the one
true witness

even the finality of holocaust
will melt away
like lowland snow

the military hardware
translated into monkey bars
where children play

the hardened postures
crumbled
like ancient statues

children will wave through the gunholes
of tanks
rumbling off to the junkyard

people will find hands
in theirs
instead of guns

learn to walk
into their gardens
instead of battle

Oh House of Israel
let's walk in the sunlit ways
of his presence

for you've been abandoned
the House of Israel
full of fortune tellers

provincial cult merchants
village idiots from the East
buying and selling the air we breathe

imitating the Philistines
the latest style of infantile
chant and handshake

and their warehouse filled with silver
and gold stuffs
beyond counting

their land full of horses
and bloated chariots
embroidered like doormen uniforms

totally superfluous
going nowhere
overly driven

their cities and roadstops thriving
crammed with idols
like supermarket shelves

in a daydream
where the ego glides freely
down the aisles

civilized slaves
to the ghost towns
they've bought in their heads

and they will lose it all
their bodies fall
dead in their tracks

in an incredible parody
of humility
bowing down to the idols

of their own toes
as they emptied their spirit
into objects of their fingers

praying to the ghosts
of themselves
and so they're abandoned

so you will hide
deep in stone
dark caves

you will pull a blanket
of dust
over your head

in a cold sweat
from a vision of your Lord
light

light you will never close
your eyes to
a Hiroshima for the blind

to what always was true
light behind us
creation before us

the false eyes of pride will look in
to find the humble man
behind him

the arrogant mind
kneels
to its earth

the highest imagination
will be shimmering sand
on that day

when only the Lord
like a blue sky
will be above us

that will be the day
a day
over the heads of all

that stands
and by its little height above the earth
is proud

feels endowed with highness
and tall words for what stands
merely upright   in its image

human or inhuman
or the giant Cedars
of Lebanon

all the upright oaks
of Bashan
all the straight-backed mountains

and high-rising hills
the skyscrapers
and sheer walls

the Super Powers
and their walls of missiles
stockpiled

the huge launching towers
of the Saturns
the incredibly tall masts

of the ancient ships of Tarshish
sailing to the edge of the world
all the beautiful craft

all the inflated art
the high-priced picture frames
and gilt-edged imitations

all the high-sounding ideas
and high-minded poses
will fade to nothing

on that clear day
will melt away
like dew on the ground

men and women
in the statues and masks
of their pride

will topple over
like carved chess pieces
in a gust of wind

the little board
on which they lived for power
swept away with sand

when only the Lord
like a blue sky
will be above us

and the idols of dark thoughts
like dreams
passed away   utterly

and men will go deep
into caves and to the depths
of darkness   holes

holes in the ground
to hide from the terrible truth
of the Lord   light

deep beauty and power
shaking the earth to its core
with the simple fact of light

men will toss away fortunes
like flaming embers
in their laps   on that day

their mind-forged status
the gold-lettered names they worship
as if their hands alone conceived them

the idols of themselves   self-inspired
the brilliant paint
on their gods and monuments

will fade in the light of that day
all the coveted possessions
become molten in their hands

and they will fling them away
to moles and bats
in a fit of inspiration

and creep into cracks
and crawl
into dark corners

in fits of desperation
clinging to stones
to petrified wood

to a cold bed to hide under
from the terrible truth
of the Lord

clear beauty and power
shaking the earth to its core
with the simple fact of light

beyond the grasp of a man
who reaches for power
and cannot hold

the breath in his nostrils
who cannot grasp it
whose sum total is less

than that little wind
blowing through him
and the naked sail of his heart.

CHAPTER 6

It was the year King Uzziah
died and the year
I saw the Lord

as if sitting in a chair
the true throne
as it was very high

so high
the train
of his robe flowed down

to fill the Temple
where I was standing
the sanctuary

seraphic beings   burning
shone around him
six wings

each had six wings
two covering the face
enfolding it

two covering the torso
and enfolding the sex
of its body

and two unfolded
in space
flying

and each was calling
to each other
and the words were saying

a chorale   a fugue
an endlessly unfolding
hymn

Holy   Holy   Holy
is the Lord   beyond
all that is

and filling the world
with the substance of light
unfolding creation

the doors the windows the foundation
were shaken
moved by each voice calling

singing out
and the House was filling
with white smoke

clouds
and I heard myself
I was saying

Oh my God!
this is the end of me
my lips are a man's

unholy
I live among men and women
who give their lips falsely

give their lips to darkness
and now my eyes are given
blinding truth

inner and outer   the one
king: Lord beyond all—
and I'm uncovered   primitive

in horror of my darkness
in terror of inhuman space
exposed to a private death

totally vulnerable on the surface
of earth's
material matter . . .

then one of the seraphim
flew toward me
a live coal in his hand

a fire from the interior
of the earth
the core of my being

it was a burning stone
from the fire
on the altar

with the priest's tongs
he reached in the holy altar
and took it

and touched my lips
with it
and he was saying

you are seeing
the purifying fire of creation
burn up your past

and abstract fear and guilt
of light   of losing yourself
your small and only light

now abstraction turns concrete
on your lips
to feel the universe

the private guilt gone
purged   lanced
like a boil

erupted around your body . . .
and I was clean
and whole

and I heard the voice
of my creator
it was saying

who will I send
to be a witness—
here am I   send me

I heard myself saying
and he said
go and say to this people

hear over and over
and understand nothing
look again and again

and again you don't see
the whole body:
of language, sound

of action, history
of memory
imagination

of matter, light
they can't even feel
the energy inside them

the material of their being
and you will make their hearts harder
like ignorant fists of matter

and their ears
heavy earrings for their mind
and their eyes shut

like a censor's eyes
before a naked soul
in front of them

their thoughts become glinting swords
to hide their narrowness
to reflect away light

they will stay out late
like stubborn children
bleary-eyed

heaven forbid they should see
with their eyes clear
hear with open ears

and understand by feeling
with that sacred metal cow
of their heart

and so be moved
to turn and become
wholly human again

how long I said how long
this shell this wall
and he was already saying

until cities have fallen
to the ground   not a house
with a person or statue standing

countryside a wasteland
until this king has driven men
away   the whole country

blown down like a primitive pile of stones
some forgotten sacred place
wiped out like royal contracts etched in sand

even the promise of a remnant of survivors
will slip from mind
like the hollow ring of a cliché

like leaves from a blighted oak
ripped in a hard wind
crumpled as the tree falls

the pages of that high pride
the record of its worldly dealings
will be smooth as a stump

the stump
the holy seed
remains.

CHAPTER 8 (1 6 – 2 3)

Roll this testimony up
in a scroll   this revelation
hidden in the inner library

of hearts still open
to the word
mind open to the ear

I am turning in   to wait for him
to look up from his reading
in the book

his face is hidden in
as if his people had become
a history book

a book ignorantly dropped
from sight
by Israel

like a mirror   absently swept away
a shattering insult
but the pages the pieces I will keep

before him
and I will look for him there
when he turns again to face us . . .

Listen to me because I
like my children
are signs of his reality

children of Israel
as it was and will be
in touch with his presence   in Zion

knowing where we come from
where we're going
where we are

on the map   the signs
our lines pass through
in the vehicle of his word

but when you hear
the consoling voices
of stylish intelligence and mass appeal

the religions of faithless men and women
trying to sell you on yourself
in the disarming pose of

generous free advice
urging you to consult ghosts
and articulate machines

the mindless testimonials
of spiritual ventriloquists
hearing the ghosts of themselves

and the assorted animal screechings
of sophisticated machines
running their metal tongues

by all means consult the machines
they are superior to us
like the dead

and listen to the motor
of your own cheap power
over others

as it drowns out self-doubt—
and why shouldn't we trust the gods
we make of ourselves—

and they will become oracles
in the dark   in the spiritual trap
of their own shadows

knocking wood
tossing coins
wishing on stars

beyond light
from the hand that put his word
in theirs   hand of light

utterly open daylight
and the warmth
of faith in its coming

they will pass through it like one
locked in the reflection of his shadow
going deeper into depression

he will walk and walk
and arrive nowhere as in a dream
going hungry

for something real
his mind growing bitter
he turns on his gods and kings

turns in on himself
cursing himself senseless
until his sky and his earth

are one
until he is floating
in the naked terror of space inside him

until he is a planet spun free
into total darkness
his mind in the grip of bottomless pain

his body desolate and airless
totally vulnerable
to the forces of darkness.

C H A P T E R 9 $(1 - 7)$

The people walking on
through darkness
will be overcome by light

those who were locked in the shadow
of death
are released by light

you have increased the nation
not in numbers
but in the joy of rebirth

they are rejoicing in beautiful weather
in the fullness of light
in a full harvest

in the simple joy of a windfall
they are carrying home the inner prize
of a deep victory   a selfless pride

like a liberation army coming home
an underground resistance coming out
their own home the spoil

openly yours
because you lifted the impenetrable lid
the selfish pride the manhole cover

the armor of all oppression
you have broken the iron grip
of repressed guilt

and we have broken through
in touch again
with the day at Midian

the original victory made new
the scrap of centuries peeled back
in the light of your presence

penetrating the manhole
of material pride   unearthing
the deep wonder of memory

preserved in the fullness
of time and space
earth we walk on and carry within

every military boot
putting its mindless scrawl
on earth's drawingboard

every uniform soaked in blood
or steeped like thoughts
in the smell of blood

will be tossed in the bonfire
and in miraculous transformation
become a fuel for peace   hearts lightened

to see a child being born
to see the future
being given to us in the moment

of wonder   to be in touch
with the inner strength of seeing
our own past lifted   to be uplifted

in the clean air of justice
to see the transforming   the shaping
that is constant reality

to feel the weight of constancy the longing
that is light as a baby
in our arms

growing in our love
the suspended sentence of guilt
our children will wear like summer clothes

and we will see it with real eyes
of earth   not in the stars
we are children of reality

struggling to give justice a name
as if it were a child
born to us

like a king
bringing the world to him
like blood flowing through the heart

as if the heart of the world's body
were on a line
descended from David

in the miracle of time
unfolding space
to realize ourselves in

in the insistence of struggle
to stay in touch   holding
a lifeline into the deep past

to touch
the infinite
within   and live

children of a free nation
struggling in the name
of Israel

to reclaim our birth
to open the window
of our ancient home

and say we're here to stay
defending justice to the stars
integrity to the light of dawn.

CHAPTER 1 4 (4 – 2 1)

One day you'll pick up this satire
of Babylon and its king
and sing:

How the storm of power
has passed
stormed off the cliff

into an endless pit
how quiet after all
the dramatic thunder

the Lord has snapped the golden crutches
of pride   cracked the whips
of despots in their own faces

who lashed the people
from an imperial seat
no country beyond reach

and now they break out singing
the whole earth is lying on its back
peacefully humming to itself

the fir trees are laughing
in the wind at you
and the cedars of Lebanon are whispering

since you lay down
the men have stopped coming
to chop us down beside you

(Oh graceful long-limbed trees
silent before the slaughter
by greedy men

who stumbled over the hills drunk
like a sunshower
that now is suddenly gone!)

the waiting room below
is all astir
at news of your coming, Babylon

all the shadows are gathering
of all the dead kings
of the world

they all stagger up to their high thrones
like ghosts of mountain goats
all the stubborn world leaders

they are all muttering they are saying
not you too
welcome to the club

so you've decided to join us
to amount to absolute zero
to bend your knee to nothing

the big parade of your pride
pushed by insatiable will
has come to the edge of the grave

to do a nose dive
all the royal trumpets
and inner noise of power

has come to play for maggots
as you stretch out on your bed of worms
and pull the blanket of worms over you

how did you fall out of bed
in heaven bright morning star
Ishtar   Lucifer

the immortal king
now reigns over sleepers
sprawled over the nations at his feet

like the shadow of The Thinker
on a plaza of flagstones
you who thought to yourself

I will climb into heaven
and set my throne on the floor
of its stars

I'll be king of the mountain
where the gods meet
utter North

I'll burst through the clouds
to make myself
god of thunder

I'll be Most High
light
will kiss my feet

but you've burst like the heaviest headstone
through the bottomless pit
utter hole

those who've been there long enough
to be accustomed to the darkness
still squint and stare at you

skeptically
like at a dim and badly painted
likeness

is this the king who made nations shake
at his feet like trembling diplomats
they say scratching the top of their skulls

who blitzed through cities
in a storm of terror
smoothing the world before him into desert

who swallowed the keys to prisons
whose bowels (they said privately) were so hard
keys came through broken in pieces

who sneered at humor
who taught the world to laugh
at humility and tears

to cry in desperate secrecy
to doubt the liberty
of their hearts in crying

who spit in the eye of kings
no foreign subject allowed to return
his last address: unknown

now all the world's kings reside
in their own plush tombs
and sleep at prominent addresses

but you've been kicked out of the mausoleum
you've been clubbed
like a Nazi collaborator

raised high above the crowd
by your heels
dressed up in royal scarlet

you and your henchmen's blood
and flung into a hole
like a horribly disfigured fetus

your head has been cracked
against the marble of your headstone
and that stone has been ground to fine powder

scattered in the wind
like the inhuman seed of your pride
unfit to be buried

in your land (incestuously exploited)
with your people (purged)
with the dignity of even a name

I will not dignify it with sound
and even your family
will be stone before it can mouth it

they will pay the sins of their father
in simple seed: their lives
extorted from the whole family

of man in the spirit of incest
in the rape of spirit itself—
let their seed be spilled

in the hole of their father
let weeds possess the earth
before that breed returns.

CHAPTER 23 (16 – 18)

TYRE, PHOENICIA

Pick up your lyre
and walk through the city
whore no one remembers

pick the strings gently
sing all your songs over
until you're remembered: desired

Once again Tyre
will be handsomely paid
like a whore

open for hire
to every self-serving kingdom
on the leering face of earth

like a royal taxi
much of the world's commerce
done inside her

its traffic
passing through her
heavily breathing

but her trade her obscene profits
will become a true vehicle
this time reopened

to the core
filled with light
nothing held back

nothing under the table
no self-reproducing capital
no closet deals

no treasures secretly hidden
but totally opened for love
for pure service   a wealth untouched

all the desperate merchandising
of life and blood and the air of a song
all the face-saving prostitution

will be a way for the Lord
the profits and losses a highway
prosperity will build a house

for those who live in his presence
who breathe in his air
there will be food for all

all human desire
will be clothed
with dignity

all will be moved
to fill their place at his table
to sing his grace.

CHAPTER 30 (8 — 23)

Come out of yourself
and take this down
print it in a book

so it can't be erased like dust
from the blackboard of people's minds
so it's engraved in their genes

because this is a stubborn race
erasing the truth in front of them
before they even read it

spoiled children: little liars
refusing to sit still
for the testimony that really frees them

saying to their open-eyed teachers: go to sleep
to their poets and prophets:
no piercing visions please

of uncensored truth
seduce us with surfaces
touch up the pain in our lives

with a little rose color
show us the movie of the future
so we can sit back and enjoy it

turn off the camera of reality
and make us like ourselves
under the glossy coats of postcards

turn off the words of the Lord
get out of the way
drown out those primitive feelings

with the upbeat popular tunes
of car radios
as we drive on landscaped expressways

over the naked parts
and around the unpainted sections
of hard times

even concentration camps
can be pruned
for respectable tourists

we can make anything
look easy
with modern minds and machines

but the Lord of Israel
has something to say
over all

you have swept the truth
under your consciousness
and let yourself hate

shamelessly
these words
I am speaking

you despise them
with the clenched teeth
you hide behind smooth lips

used to deceive
and to set an example of trust
in cynical salesmanship

and moral bankruptcy
relying on the cheap paper
of politics

the secret darkness
you wall in yourselves
is a fatal flaw

a fault line
nobody sees and easily forgets
under intense pressure

a trace of steam
a slight rumbling
is vaguely there until the

instant shock
the earth cracking as simply
as a china knickknack

knocked from the shelf
in the deeper quake
of his justice

your inflated careers
mere figurines
of rigid selfhood

will fall like tiny porcelains
from a tower
bursting totally apart

not a piece recognizable
mere traces of fine powder
as total as the sudden shocking

explosion of a zeppelin
not even a bolt or propeller
left for salvage

not even a photograph
a scrap of paper—
so irretrievably present

so decisive
is his presence
in his speaking

these are his words
precise pieces of language
making up the one

over Israel
over all
in my speaking

a secureness is found
as one slows down
a quiet confidence

in hearing and seeing
building strength
to open oneself

in the strength of trust
but not this people
only their mouths are open

saying not us
we've got fast horses
we can escape any danger

and they will escape
and they will ride
into the jaws of danger

saying we are so clever
as the teeth flash
behind them   unclenched

in a terrible smile
one of those smiles
will set a thousand fleeing

ten bared lips
and all will be running
as if they could escape themselves

as if they could escape
up the self-made mountain
of themselves

until what is left of them
stands free in the breeze
like a flag left on a mountain

like a warning light still flashing
in the wind-racked unearthly solitude
of a deserted runway

from some forgotten war
a tin flag in a strange wind
left behind on the moon

but even now   as then
the Lord is waiting
to embrace you

you will open to him
as pure mountain air
totally surrounding you in an embrace

there is a just voice speaking
in the quiet strength of those
listening

to his presence unfolding
around them
like a scroll of overwhelming poetry

you are survivors of the future
in Jerusalem in Israel
your tears have fallen like rain

in the desert of the past
where he hears you crying
he responds in the flowing

of your own voice
and though your mouth is dry
from the suffering you've recorded

and your hand weak from the journey
from the inner severing
of the hands you've had to let go

the teacher you've carried deep within
in the seat of your conscience
will come out

passing memory and thought
and the huge mirror of imagination
to stand in front of you

in the light of your eyes
your teacher your life
in front of you

you will see yourself
alive in the future
you will come out to meet it

and the words will come over you
a voice will be there
that was within you

and your ears will embrace it
and your arms will reach out
and sweep away the precious idols

your poets will be prophets
vehicles on the one road
in front of you

a real road
and when your mind wanders
they will call you back

to the present
to the space and time
we create together: *dialogue*

of creation
wind and rain
on the open faces

pleasing the deep roots
cleansing the leaves
that bear his message

you will bite into the sweet
miraculous rainbow
of real fruit

and spit out the bitter fruit of self-made power
the dry self-worship
greased with gold and silver

worked up like sexual fantasies
into illusions of success
over the dead bodies of others

those dreams will be wiped out
real for only an instant
returned to the earth as manure is

enriching it for the rain
he sends
to wash away the decaying past

to open the infinite eyes
of the living past:
the seeds we plant

as each living thing does
and so there is always bread
and meat

and if we let our eyes fully open
to ripen in the air
we are planted in

we can grow up and see
beyond it
into the infinite universe of stars.

CHAPTER 4 O (1 — 1 1)

Console my people
comfort your people
my Lord   speaking

in my voice   saying
speak to the heart
of Jerusalem tenderly

in a voice embracing her
call to her
that her exile is over

come home
the sentence is over
that knocked the voice out of her

her guilt has been paid
into the firm hand
that is the Lord's

into which she paid more than herself
and now that hand of justice
is still open

to support her
listen a voice is calling
to open a road through the desert

clear a highway for the Lord
straight through the desert
and through your throat that is parched

deep stone valleys
you struggle through
will be filled in

lifted to your feet
to make a smooth way
a plain rolled out before you

stubborn obstacles
mountains and hills
will be swept away like dust

and a new carpet laid out
level
for all flesh to see

and to walk on together
to feel the firm reality
of his way

spread before us
direct and clear
as words spoken through air

touch all that is there
and we will see the Lord clearly
as these words from him

a voice said speak
and a voice said
what should I say

say
all flesh is grass
and the reality of love is there

wild flowers in the field
and all flesh blooms
no longer than a flower

the grass shrivels and dies
the flowers curl up to paper
in the wind

that is an undying breath
of the Lord
surely the people are grass

grass shrivels flowers fade
but the word of our God
stands in the wind forever

stand up prophets and speak to Jerusalem
your tired litany reawakens as poetry
embrace her with good news

speak to her
heart of Zion
from the top of a mountain

let your voice rise to the mountains
with the strength of love
fearless headline of truth

let all the cities of Israel see
and hear the true
Here I am!

Here is your God
here
see how he is strength itself

and vision is his arm
ruling hearts
with the power of feeling justice

to see we are here
we are our own reward
his words make us a priceless vehicle

carrying his work forward
in our arms like books
that is the air we breathe

and we are carried in it
like lambs
gently breathing

in the arms of a shepherd
in the law of life itself
in the justice of air itself

we look around and
there are pastures
and leaning against his arm new mothers

giving suck
and he is leading the ewes
to water.

Listen to this vision
and know my poorest servant
my student most despised

overcomes   uplifted and held
above material honor
a tower an immovable mountain

a model of strength that makes
faces of worldly power pale   masks
over wills of mere steel

the many who turned aside in their superior air
appalled at his uncivilized
state his wild appearance

as if he had no human parents
as if he came from beyond humanity
out of some ancient ruins

a wild-eyed student
starved and sickly
from a condemned ghetto

those many appalled nations
"civilized" and "progressive"
will find their eyes glued

and their imaginations riveted
on him
the mouths of world leaders

will fall open
in amazed silence
before their own ignorance

of something so real
their lips turning to rubber
before their false education

their ears burning
with the fact
of what they've never listened to.

CHAPTER 5 3

Is there anyone to believe
what we've listened to
as we report it

who is there
who's actually seen the Lord's
arm around the shoulders

of the despised   this richness
incredible support
freely given to him

who would have believed
seeing we were as unconscious of him
among us as a common tree

a weed tree in a lot
junk-strewn in a poor section
of the city

what could have been there
to attract us   no handsomeness
nothing to divert the eye

how could we even turn our heads
for something so poor in our eyes
so uninspiring

he was a thing rejected
despised for being human
in an offensive suit of clothes

the clothes of suffering
a shirt of pain
a cloak of sorrow

a coat the solid color
of loss   worldly indifference
like leprosy written across his face

so densely it hurt to look
as if we'd only see
ourselves reflected in it

as in a dense layer of dust
over a window
in an ancient place we've long forgotten

we don't want to remember
we loathe that place
we despise weakness

and he meant nothing to us
a blight on our existence
we couldn't even condone his existence

but it was our
loss and our
pain he bore

our hidden fear and indifference
he wore
openly for us

while we wrote him off as beneath us
as an example of God's vengeance
as being even our own self-vindication

he was punished
tortured by disease
to condone our fear

hidden under a worldly cloak
thrown over our unconscious
we've swept it out of sight

we wrote it off
with the hurt and loss
as if struggle and pain

were not a human bond
a mirror in which to see
ourselves

not an unreflecting
stone
fear symbol

but he was shattered
for our heart of stone
he was locked in ghettoes

for our hidden guilt
and we are made human
together

in the punishment and contempt
he wears in the world
on this earth for us

in black and blue
our eyes can see it
and we are healed by that seeing

he makes us real
we were all victims
we were all sheep

we strayed   we were lost
we wandered away
lost in ourselves

we were all nations
servants of our own
interests

we made our own selfish way
slavishly alone
each with our own patch of lust

in the unconscious pasture
of self-indulgence
trespassers of spirit

silent accomplices of thugs
on the highway of feeling
that is the Lord's

that is his word
and the Lord has chosen
his servant to carry it

a burden of pain on his naked back
beyond power of men to lay on him
it is the guilt of us all

made real
the guilt inside us
the abyss we were losing

our richness of feeling in
and now we see how cheaply
we've papered over loss

how openly it's borne
beyond our power to pay
he was a low animal in our eyes

a carrier of disease
and we treated him
lower than dogs

but he didn't open his mouth
for bitterness
he was open to the core

he was a lamb
led to slaughter
he was an innocent sheep

as his coat is shorn from him
but he was human   he suffered
and like a lamb his mouth didn't open

out of bitterness
and he was led away
stripped of his rights

shorn of his humanity
not a shred of justice for him
not a mouth opened for him

he was deported
he was sentenced
out of existence itself

like a nation marked for death
he was led into the fire
of bitter hatred

he was led alive
into ovens   he burned
as indifferently to the world as an ordinary lamp

turned on at evening
a lamp of skin
and no one gave it thought

he was a flame
lit in the darkness of terror
he was a light

to the truly guilty
those who deserved to be lost
in their own land

in their own bitter darkness
in the abyss
of their hidden guilt

my own people were blind
but his eyes were true
suffering the world for them

and the world gave him a grave
unmarked like a criminal's
like a mass grave

the way cattle are buried
the way refuse is disposed of
the way a rich man

orders cut flowers
like common flowers crushed beside a highway
he was nothing he was in the way

he was banned from sight   victimized
by a decadent justice
a worldly masquerade

of men dressed up in power
he was naked   innocent of crime
not guilty of even a common lie

but the Lord allowed him to feel
pain   to be open
to injustice as to disease

to be vulnerable as an animal
given in spirit of sacrifice
a faith in a human future

and out of that death march
through the fire
out of that holocaust

out of the deepest abyss
beyond torture and despair
out of sheer hell furnaces

he comes through
piercing through the guilt
deep fear and self-contempt

of all the world
because he gave himself whole
persistently human

transcending spears of bitterness
and for his pain
the pain of all creation

he will have children again
and he will see them
as sure as they will feel

his soul
and the deep consolation spoken
in the openness allowed

by the Lord
by his hand
through his words

through the pure insistence
to bear his words
in human hands   his servant

out of the massive depths of pain
into the daylight
of a living nation

that is his future illuminated
as real and warm as a body
lit by the color of feeling

my servant an example
lighting the steps up
from deep depression beneath the surface

everywhere
a struggle for the merest foothold
in the mass of people and nations

and out of the inhuman scars the clawing
he made his heart a vessel
out of the storm the raging

of primitive pride
he carried my justice a lightness
in his nameless heart   open

a room without walls
room for the lowest and highest
guilt   all that is borne within

and without: the world is his
to share with the richest nations
in the present

I make his future present
and the mouths of worldly power
fall open in awe

at the beauty
the utter reality laid bare
of life itself

because he opened his heart
totally   putting it in the hands
of death

speaking straight through a transparent life
from his soul
and his nakedness was a menace

he was judged for his skin
what is visible to the lowest
a disgrace to worms

dressed in material
of pride
a crime to those human eyes

locked up in themselves
and he was given the final clothes
of death   dust of the earth

and he wore the deaths
of those with murder in their hearts
and the criminal thoughts

of all in self-hating prisons
and he was stripped of his self
for sheer integrity

of the deeper language
of creation
and as he was scarred

in his openness
beyond worldly recognition
for the self-debased to see

their disease in him
and as he was crushed by weight
of their hidden guilt revealed

he heard it is the creator speaking
words of life
you will survive by them

your voice: lightness of breath itself
clothe the cold and hidden
hearts of stone

and warm in the dark
the unborn   vulnerable as you were
your light into the future.

C H A P T E R   5 8   (1 — 1 2)

Open up and speak from the heart
a voice rushing through you
startling the air

a lover
rushing to the side
of a wounded mate

wind opening the door
of a deserted mountain cabin
a wounded mountain ram

lift your voice
like a horn
to your lips

calling to my people
they are guilty
they are wounded

hiding their wounds
inflicted on each other
within   in pride

indifference and self-righteousness
shout it openly   jar the doors and windows
of this House of Israel

because they're still looking for me
daily   finding pride
in looking like they're searching

all dressed up
in clothes of righteousness
like a moral nation

wearing the moral law on their sleeve
and acting
as if their integrity depends on it

as if they're beyond acting
so may approach me
like a judge over their house

asking for direction
in the immoral streets
anxious for approval of their way

anxious children
impatient to please
tugging at the sleeve of justice

why are we fasting a day
if you won't take a moment
to notice they ask

why are we humbling ourselves
dressed in mourning
sacrificing body

baring soul
if you won't know it
answer us

here it is
you ask for answered prayers
when you won't stop to think

thinking with your feet
carrying you to the marketplace
only of yourself

how to further your business
on the shoulders
of others

thinking with your stomach
the day you're fasting
an empty stomach-mind

unable to get past yourself
pushing and shoving
unable to stand still inside

turning the intensity of this day
up like metallic car radios
playing mindless words and music

geared to desperation
to turning a profit on silence
an assembly line of minutes

on which you turn out
cheap images of yourself
material to digest with an iron stomach

making you more irritable
grasping for words of spirit
to swallow like bitter pills

to make yourself feel better
about turning your soul
inside out like another pocketbook

turning openness around
with a gun at its back
like a desperate criminal

"sacrificing" your precious time
at the primitive altar
with the money of your ritual donations

turning on a figment of imagination
in a pagan death-cult act of "self-sacrifice"
in which you offer a hollow shell

going through mechanical motions
impressing hollow religious phrases
on metal

you fast with a vengeance
pushing past the inner voice
too bruised to rise and be heard

is this a day for rising
standing in my presence
expecting a reward

for physical sacrifice   for your fasting
bowing heads like royal footmen
like rows of bulrushes

parting for the heavy prow of ritual
self-serving ghost ship
with its real cargo of slaves

instead of your soul you save
face by fasting
and I can't see through *that?*

wake up to a day
beyond acting
for yourself

the Lord's voice speaks
for itself:
act for others

not with faces but hands
opening
locks of injustice

sophisticated knots
tied mentally and physically
around the poor and powerless

like a harness
to break their spirit
free them . break the locks

cut the reins of oppression
rise to the occasion
fast to free man's spirit

make a day for opening
your cupboards
sharing with the poor

open your house your heart
to the homeless
open your eyes

instead of filling your stomach
instead of harnessing the weak for it
look at the hopeless around you

put your hand through that invisible curtain
and throw a coat around their shoulders
those are men and women

flesh like you   desperate and blind
outside the walls you've built to hide in—
the _otherness_ you reach for is _there_

all around you
nakedly human
to a soul undressed by kindness

bare hands
untying the cloak of self-serving pride
and wrapping it around a naked body

and then all around you
as sudden as light
to eyes opening in the morning

the light inside you breaks open
as certain and irrevocable
as dawn

you will see yourself
healed by a human warmth
in the reality of daylight

a sky clearing over you
like new flesh over a wound
your body will be whole

and you will see it in the light
of others   revealed
in care for the hurt you've left behind

and openness to those you find
on the way of your future
like lost memories of your creator

memory repressed
oppressed   dispossessed
now yours from which to speak

sing out openly
and the Lord returns
your voice

call into empty space
for help
and he answers "Here I am"

and if you open
the locks of injustice around you
rip open the curtain of suspicion

remove the ring from the finger of status
you point at the poor
and open your mind to them

removing the insults from your tongue
and if you open your hand
dropping your body's show of pride

showing compassion sharing your gift of life
pouring the milk of your kindness
for the starved and hopeless

then the light inside you
will rise like the sun
from the dead of night

and the depression hidden within you
will walk out openly a child
free under an afternoon sky

the Lord will be behind you
always around you
water in the desert of your need

meat and strength for your bones
and over you gentle rains
your life a fruitful garden

a mountain spring
always running
under a clear sky

and many from among you will walk out
to build on your ruins
firming the shaken doors and windows

reaffirming the ancient foundations
of your ancestors
on earth

and you will walk out
in the universe
deep in the firmament

building from the ruins
of planetary bodies
renewing the foundation

of the changing universe
continually
by your presence

water of your body
unchanging air
of your soul

you will be spoken of
openly and everywhere
as discoverer of lost ways

restorer of faded memories
nurse to broken dreams
surveyor of a universal highway

landscaper of sandswept paths irrigator of deserts
plasterer of broken walls rebuilder of broken defenses
archaeologist of morning

making a world
to live in   secure
in the infinite light of reality.

The Lord speaks
this way
the sky

and all ways behind it
is a royal seat for me
space

is where I rest
and the earth my footrest
in time

where could you build a house
for me
where a place

especially for me to rest
as if I would sleep or abide
there   or there

when I made all this
all of it comes from my hand
all that is came into being

from me
my Lord
is speaking

but I look at man especially
for the man or woman oppressed
poor and powerless

when he knows he is
brokenhearted and
filled with humility

his body trembling with care
open to the others
to my words.

Jeremiah

THE ORIGINAL *Jeremiah* was shaped by Baruch, and his autobiography takes up much of it. Baruch was the prophet Jeremiah's secretary, supposedly setting down his master's words. One can't help but feel that Baruch's textual fidelity includes a measure of respect for his reader: he gives us a range of Jeremiah's moods, sometimes raw, sometimes elaborated with great sophistication. It helps to imagine Jeremiah in his lamentation as a soul musician: when transcribed, the illusion of spokenness to Jeremiah's blues texts becomes artful in Baruch's subtle settings.

Later, other poets in the school of Jeremiah added passages and chapters to the book, while perhaps editing earlier portions. The chapter from which I've translated appears written by one of these later poets, based upon some lines attributed to the original Jeremiah. The vision of a return from exile seems to have been written in retrospect, long after the Babylonian captivity that Jeremiah experienced. It's a poignant vision for a reader who knows of the real hardship and poverty encountered in the return. In fact, few returned to Jerusalem at first, and this passage was probably meant to be read by those still living in Babylon. Alternatively, if it was written in the following century, it would be directed to those who had already assimilated the shock of returning. They would have accepted this text with a fondness toward an earlier, more idyllic age (as an Israeli poet today might look back fondly on the romantic idealism of the Zionist pioneers).

The key to the vision—one that later, hard-bitten realists might still accept—is the promise of children (and a new audience), an exaggerated echo of Abraham's original blessing. As God remembers Ephraim (a term of endearment for the northern kingdom of Israel); as Jeremiah remembers a mother of Israel, Rachel; and as we remember the words, "there is new life for your labor, remembrance/ in the presence of children"—so we become aware, as readers "listening," that *we* were the children. Just as Ephraim and Rachel are breathing presences in Jeremiah's poetry, the blessing is redeemed in the eyes and ears of "the children alive."

❧ *Jeremiah* ☙

Listen to words the Lord has spoken:
A people discovered grace
when they had run away

a consoling treasure
when they had escaped an enslaving power
into the desert

immeasurable richness in front of their eyes
opening their hearts and minds
when you had looked only for rest, Israel

the Lord reveals his words to me
as he was then, in that desert
ages ago, saying

a love that lasts forever
I revealed to you
and you always will carry that loving-kindness

the love that drew you to me
will rebuild your nation
will draw you home, dear Maiden Israel

again you will fasten on timbrels
leading the dance   keeping time
to the rhythm of seasons

again you will clothe the mountains with vineyards
the hills of Shomron will sparkle
with the jewelry of vines

and you will live to pluck the fruit
to raise it to your lips
to praise it, singing

for there will be a day
when watchmen on the hills of Ephraim
will shout, the way is clear

we may go up to Zion
the mountain of vision
walking in the presence of the Lord

for these are the Lord's words:
raise a song to your lips for Jacob
let the startled nations hear it

let their watchmen turn to it
on every hilltop listening post
of the world

let it be music to their ears:
am Yisrael chai
the people of Israel live

I am bringing them back from the north
and gathering them
from the ends of the earth

look, the blind and the lame are returning
women heavy with child, and yes
even those already feeling birth pangs

a great congregation is coming
weeping openly, and among them little cries
of newborn infants—sweet and gracious tears

and I will lead them beside rushing waters
on fertile ground, on soil so smooth
not a foot will stumble on the way

their path is straight, clear before them
for I am Israel's father
Ephraim my firstborn son

nations of the world, listen
to the word that is the Lord's
turn and tell it to the islands

islands, send it to the coasts
the one who scattered Israel
is a shepherd who never sleeps

and will bring them back
gathering his flock tenderly
unchanging as the sea

for the Lord has redeemed Jacob
paid the ransom into the worldly hand
that was too strong for him

they will come home with songs
singing from the mountaintop
that is Zion

the land will be beautiful in their eyes
the earth's goods abundant
in their hands

the fullness of their hearts
will reap wheat
and wine and oil

flocks of sheep
giving birth to healthy lambs
vigorous herds of cattle

and the people will take root
thrive and stretch themselves
like a watered garden

they will not be confined
not imprisoned in exile again
not steeped in sadness

the maiden will dance unashamedly
young men and old men
will join in together

I will turn their sighing
into breaths of excitement
their sadness into blushes of joy

and they will relax by fountains
of imagination, clearing the air
of dank grief

their mourning changed into music
of birds alighting in trees, by windows
thrown open to new mornings

the priests will have their arms full
with gifts for the sacrifice
the hunger of the people will be filled

with the goodness of the world
and their hearts thrown open
to hear these words again

like fresh air to comfort them
for the Lord has given his word—
just as now you hear his words:

listen, a voice sobbing in Ramah
bitter weeping, open
inconsolable

Rachel mourns her children
refusing all comfort, all soothing
all her hope gone blind:

her children gone—
yet these are the Lord's words:
your voice will cease its weeping

your eyes brighten behind the tears
that dissolve into crystal-clear vision
of the children alive

returning home
from the lands of enemies
from beyond anguish to hope revived

vision is your reward
there is new life for your labor, remembrance
in the presence of children, eyes wide open

turning to the future
that is also yours
within the borders of a reality

and beyond them your descendants
are walking freely
by the strength of an unfailing imagination

an unbroken integrity
a listening   dedicated
to the words that bade them live.

As I have heard Ephraim crying
as I hear him rocking in grief:
my heart has been trained

like a wild bull, an unbroken calf
all my desire set on returning
remembering in the turning

trusting in the memory
for you are the Lord
and were always my God

and when I opened my eyes in exile
my stomach turned, I knew my loss
and when I repented and learned

to bear the burden
and when I knew I had been tested
I broke down, I struck my forehead

aware of my arrogance
ashamed of the ignorance
blinding my youth

and I lived to face it
to blush with the disgrace
to embrace my past

Is Ephraim not my dear one
says the Lord
dear as an only child

that whenever I speak of him
I am filled with remembering
and my heart goes out to him

to welcome him back
to receive him with love
with mercy, says the Lord

mark your path well
plant guideposts and road marks
set your desire by the highway

your thoughts to the road leading home
turn back on it, my Maiden Israel
come back to these your cities.

Zechariah

COMPOSED during the period of return from Babylonian exile, in
the sixth and fifth centuries B.C., the imagery used by the poet
reflects a cosmopolitan influence in its representation of a heavenly
court. The poet also revives older Jewish imagery, as in the repre-
sentation of the Temple Menorah. Yet here the Menorah has
become a powerful image in a dream while the heavenly court is
suffused with down-to-earth details, including political attitudes
toward the governing head, Zerubbavel. It appears that Zechariah
was more a poet than a prophet—or that a sophisticated poet in
his camp set his works in writing. There are probably several poets
who composed different chapters of the book, some less sublime
than the one I've chosen.

In this portion of *Zechariah,* the coming together of state
(symbolized by Zerubbavel) and religion (symbolized by Joshua)
echoes back to earlier mergers, starting with the ark in Sinai built
by Moses and the temple built by Solomon (where the creation of
the Menorah is first described). There are parallels as well with
earlier prophets, particularly Ezekiel. Yet this poet in the circle of
Zechariah is different—he has learned complex literary techniques
during his stay in Babylon. His dialogues between God, prophet,
and interpreting angel encompass a literary style that conceals
nuances of criticism toward both politics and religion.

The night visions are hallucinatory scenes and even though
a prophetic symbology is counterpointed by political allegory, the
poet's craft has overtaken the prophet's. Most biblical scholars

miss the poetry for the allegory and pursue meanings secondary to the text's imaginative power. It is more likely that in *Zechariah* we are in the presence of a renaissance in Jewish poetry, a poetry of Exile that will culminate in *Jonah*.

✤ *Zechariah* ✤

(2 : 1 4 — 4 : 7)

Sing like a skylark
happy being home
daughter of Zion

because I am coming
to join you
with the sky you hoped for

over you
sky of your deepest dream
infinite sky

of reality
you dared to see
in the midst of a fogbound world

I will be in the midst of you
as true as your eyes
see through a clear blue sky

and I will be inside of you
as you were open to me   light
in a world suppressed in darkness

leadenly earthbound
giants in their mirror
hearing only themselves

and the gargoyles of their unconscious
but light is the voice of your creator
breaking through you

in the midst of the world
and many nations will see it
dawn breaking on that day

all will join me in the light
of reality   warm
beneath an infinite wing

and you will know my breath is sent
the man who is speaking to you
by the Lord our creator

who will breathe in Israel
once again enfolding his daughter
Zion in the holy land

holding Jerusalem
small reflection
in the pupil of an eye

beholding him again
beneath an azure sky
calm inside

be quiet be still
all people of flesh
before the Lord

a sky of promise is unfolding
before us
the horizon expands

to include earth and sky
and the small voice within
will break out singing.

Then the Lord allowed me to see
in a vision
the high priest Joshua

in a court in heaven
the judge the Lord's angel
(the word for divine agent)

to his right the satan
(the word for accuser)
accusing him

and the word of the Lord
⸱ said to the satan
May the Lord reject your words hard accuser

the Lord who chooses Jerusalem
rejects your flood of venom
this man is but an ashen stick

plucked from the fire—
Joshua's clothes were filthy
as he stood before the angel—

who was saying to those in the heavenly court
take off his poor and filthy clothes
and turning to him was saying: look

I have removed your guilt
and dress you in clean robes—
and then it was I who was saying:

let them put a clean turban on his head!
and they did
and he was splendidly dressed

as the Lord's angel watched
then to Joshua slowly said
(matching the depth of his attention)

these are the words of the Lord
if you will walk through your life
in my ways

and keep my presence there
in the people's life
you will be head of my house

and present in my court
free to come and go
in this heavenly court

listen Joshua   high priest
you and your new pioneers
are signs of the growth coming

you are like new shoots
and I will bring you
a new branch a new line

the man growing from my promise
as from a root
in the promised land

look at this stone it has eyes
I reveal to Joshua
seven facets seven eyes

cornerstone of a new day
on which I engrave
the living inscription the promise

that on that one day
I will remove
the dirty clothes and guilt

from the shoulders of this land
and in your lightness
you will see every man your neighbor

and call to him
(the words of the Lord are speaking)
come sit on this good earth with me

beneath my fig tree
(each will be truly at home)
and my ripening vine.

·   ·   ·

Then the angel returned
startling me with words
as if life was a dreamy silent movie

until an angel spoke to me
saying what do you see
and my words like an unblinking camera

showed me a golden menorah
a golden bowl above it
brimming with oil

fed from two olive trees
standing on each side
there are seven lights

fed by the golden oil
so that it's always lit
by the trees

seven golden flames
lit by trees
like a blazing fountain

then I turned to the angel
speaking again
in words of conversation

what are these things my Lord
I've described
through the camera of vision

you don't know how to read then
what you've written?
spoke the angel that was there

conversing with me
and I was saying
no my Lord

then he answered
and was saying
these words

this is the word of the Lord
(immediate vision)
to Zerubbavel the governor

not by force
not by power
but by my spirit

says the Lord
what are you
worldly mountain

of all material things
and earthbound forces
compared to Zerubbavel?

you are nothing a false shrine
leveled to the ground
and he will hold up the crowning headstone

that was highest once beneath the sky
and it will be a cornerstone
of azure

and all will step back deeply in awe
of pure beauty
singing the grace of spirit.

Jonah

MOST COMMENTATORS, religious and secular, strain to place *Jonah* among the books of the Prophets. It fits most naturally as a critique: a sympathetic but intricate satire of the Jewish prophets (a precursor of the anti-heroic genre that is typical of great cultures in exile). Later parallels abound, particularly in modern Yiddish literature.

The author is worldly, and in the manner of biblical poetry the text appropriates older verses about a prophet Jonah into a new tale. But only an outsider among prophets could unite so many critical dimensions in one narrative. At the time of writing, in the fifth century B.C., the women of the elite classes educated in Babylon might hold a cautionary view of the increasingly male conventions of prophecy. *Jonah* exhibits a wry critique of these conventions.

The institution of official prophecy would find itself in turmoil as a result of exile, and an exaggerated backlash against the old fixture of women prophets would have been likely—and also require countering. At the same time, new schisms between elite and priestly classes would have arisen. The educated woman who probably wrote *Jonah* nevertheless sympathizes with honest piety. She is perhaps related to ancestral women prophets, or to a male prophet held in derision (of which there were many after the nation's downfall)—or even more aptly, to a family of the ruling class under criticism from religious quarters.

Like a typical book of a prophet, the book begins with the call to witness. But in place of Jonah's words, we're suddenly in the realm of narrative, as the prophet's failings are characterized as bluntly as any common man's. This is especially surprising because Jonah is, after all, the recipient of a call. An essential difference is established between this book and the legends of similar date recalled in the collections of Midrash. Even more extraordinary than the fantastic imagery of fish, plant, and naïve Ninevites, is that this is prophecy *about* prophecy.

The primary commentary in *Jonah* is on biblical language itself, and the customs of prophecy and prayer. The elegiac language in Jonah's psalm at the bottom of the sea—and within the roundly figurative fish belly—serves as caricature to self-possessed prophecy. Everywhere, literalism is under attack. Consider the Hebrew word for "great"—this same word is applied to the fish, to the city of Nineveh, and to the hurricane. The verbatim quality of the diction in *Jonah* is subverted by the context the poet presents, beginning with Jonah's error in taking God's call too literally (as if he could escape it by crossing a border, which is what the words required of him in the call to Nineveh).

The poet of *Jonah* is calling on men and prophets to listen to themselves self-critically. It's not the castor-oil plant that is the object lesson in the last chapter, but imagination itself. We have to absorb the irony of the imagery in order to grasp the emotional core—as Jonah feels kinship with the plant. At the core is the representation of a mothering God (cried out to, from a womblike belly) and the deity's way of speaking to poets in their own language (the language of both poetry and creation).

Jonah uses some terms in common with *Isaiah* and turns them inward, personalizing them. The familiar word for "call" also becomes "cry in its ear," since it's a word depicting *human* conversation (it's the same word used by the captain of the ship in the mundane act of waking the napping Jonah). The most emphatic contrast is in Jonah's usage of it, within the fish belly, and the impersonal utilization of it in the command to cry to Nineveh. This is one of many instances in which the poetic language parallels the drama of Jonah finding his identity in listening to—rather than separating from—the mothering God who perhaps resides within him.

❧ *Jonah* ❧

CHAPTER 1

And the word of God came to the prophet Jonah
saying to him, Jonah ben Amittai: rise
go to Nineveh, the great city
and cry in its ear
because its hard heart stands out before me
like an open sore

Jonah rose, but to go instead
west to Tarshish: far away
out of the Lord's presence
to the ends of the earth, for good measure

Jonah went down to foreign Jaffa
found a ship going all the way to Tarshish
bought a one-way ticket
(paid in cash on demand)
went below like any other passenger
as the crew set sail for distant Tarshish
away from the Lord, out of his demanding presence

But the Lord threw a great wind
over the sea—a hurricane so great
the ship thought she'd be broken to pieces
all the sailors were scared to death
each trembling soul
crying to one god or another
then throwing all the cargo overboard
to lighten the load

Meanwhile Jonah, having already lain down
in the hold below, was fast asleep

the captain himself came down to him
and cried in his ear: what does this mean
this sleep of ignorance—rise
cry to your god
perhaps the god will turn his ear
and kindly spare us our death

Among the sailors each consulted his neighbor
and agreed: we must cast lots
revealing the source of this bitter fortune
so they cast lots, fortune continuing to unfold
as Jonah drew the cast lot

Turning to him they said: now tell us—
now that you've brought your bitter fortune
on all our heads—why are you here?
where did you come from?
what country, what people
do you belong to?

And he answered: I am a Hebrew
and I tremble before the Lord
God in heaven, creator of this sea
as well as dry land

And the men were struck with a great terror
their lips trembling as they asked: what
is this bitter fortune you've created?
because the men already knew Jonah's fear
of the Lord—of being in his presence
he has told them as much

And they asked: what can we do
for you, that might calm the sea
around us? for the sea was growing
into a great hurricane

And he said: lift me up, like a sacrifice
throw me into the sea
this will calm the sea for you
it was on account of me, I'm sure
this great hurricane surrounds you

But the men desperately rowed for dry land
yet couldn't—the sea grew even more
into a great hurricane

And they cried to the Lord
Please Lord hear us
we don't want to die for this man's soul
along with him—please don't hold us guilty
of spilling his blood into the sea
for you are the Lord who has created
this fortune unfolding here

And they lifted Jonah up, like a sacrifice
and threw him into the sea

Suddenly the sea stopped its raging
the men trembled in awe
a great fear of the Lord engulfed them
right there
they slaughtered a sacrifice, sacrificing to him
they cried vows, vowing to him.

CHAPTER 2

And a great fish was waiting
the Lord had provided
to swallow Jonah

And Jonah was a long time
within the fish body
three days three nights

and Jonah prayed to the Lord
within the mothering fish body—
he prayed to his God, saying

I cried out within my despair
I called to the Lord and he answered me
I implored him within the belly of death itself

Yet he heard my voice—
I was flung into the abyss
swept into the sea's bottomless heart

Devoured by rivers
all your waves and walls of water
fell over me

And I was saying I am lost
cast away, driven out
of your presence, from before your eyes

How will I see
your holy Temple again
if I am gone?

Water was all around me
penetrating to my soul: I was almost gone
devoured by a flood

Seaweeds were tangled
around my head
I sank to the depths

I went down to the roots
of mountains
the earth shut her gates

Behind me
it was the end of the world
for me—and yet

From destruction you brought me to life
up from the pit
Lord my God

My soul was ebbing away within me
but I remembered the Lord
and my prayer came up to you

Up to your holy Temple
as if I were there
in your presence

Those who admire mists of illusion
to hide their fears
abandon the compassion of openness

But I with a thankful voice, not fearing
will make of sacrifice a thanksgiving
I will pay with gladness every vow I make

It is the Lord who delivers us
alive
he is the captain of our praises

I will pay my fare gladly
I am his
precious cargo

And the Lord spoke to the fish
and it vomited Jonah out
onto dry land.

CHAPTER 3

And the word of God came to the prophet Jonah
for the second time, saying: rise
go to Nineveh, the great city
and cry in its ear
with the words I give you to cry

Jonah rose, and went to Nineveh
as the word of God had said
now Nineveh was a great city
even in God's eyes—so wide
it took three whole days to walk across

And Jonah walked right in
walking one day's worth into it
then cried out, saying
just forty days more
and Nineveh falls

And the people of Nineveh believed the Lord
they cried out, calling for a fast
then all of them dressed in sackcloth
from the greatest on down
to the smallest

And God's word reached the King of Nineveh
and he rose from his throne
removed his robes

covered himself in sackcloth
and sat down in ashes

And it was shouted throughout Nineveh
as the word of the king
and all his great men, saying
of man or beast
of flock or herd
none shall taste food or graze
none will feed, none drink water

They will cover themselves in sackcloth
the man and the beast
crying out to the Lord
with all his might—
and will not bear injustice

And each will turn away
from his hardhearted way
from the grip of illusion
that frees his hands from violence only—
who knows, the god may turn
and repent
and turn from his burning wrath
and kindly spare us our death

And the Lord saw
what they had made of themselves
how they turned from their bitter ways
and the Lord repented from the bitterness he said
that they would bear
he didn't make them bear it.

CHAPTER 4

And this appeared like a bitter justice to Jonah
a great bitterness grew inside him
it hurt him deeply

And he prayed to the Lord, saying
Oh Lord, wasn't this the exact word and vision
I had always delivered and known you by
when I was still in my own country?
this is exactly why
I wanted to leave your presence
for Tarshish, before you would call me
a second time
because I knew you as a gracious God
compassionate, long-suffering
and of great kindness
and would repent bitterness

Now, Lord, take my soul from me
for me it is a good thing to be dead
and leave the presence of the living
and the Lord said
can it be a good thing
that you are hurt so deeply?

And Jonah left the city
walking all the way through it
and beyond it on the other side
where he sat down, east of Nineveh
having made a *sukkah* for himself in the desert
to sit in the shade, in the fragile booth
until what is made of the city
is revealed

And the Lord God had provided
a castor-oil plant, making it grow large
up over Jonah's head, a cooling shadow
to save him from bitterness
to soothe him

And Jonah began to feel happy
with the castor-oil plant
a great happiness came over him
changing his mood

And the Lord had provided
a worm in the night
and by the time darkness had risen away
it attacked the castor-oil plant
which wilted, was already dry

And then, the sun already shining
the Lord had provided a desert east wind
blistering
and the sun grew fierce, attacking
Jonah's head, he was falling
into a daze, wishing he was dead
already, saying
for me it is a good thing to be dead

And the Lord said to Jonah
can it be a good thing
that you are hurt so deeply
and because the castor-oil plant
no longer can soothe you?
and Jonah was saying
it is a good thing to be hurt deeply
until I am dead like it

And the Lord said: *you*
may feel compassion, may identify
with the castor-oil plant
for which you did not labor
to bring here, did not provide for its growing
into a great plant—a sudden child of a night
yet in one night it was gone

And may I not feel compassion
for Nineveh, the great city
which has grown up here with more than
a hundred and twenty thousand men and women
all of them innocent of knowing
the difference between right (the hand that provides)
and left—and likewise
many, many animals?

The Story's Call

RUTH

ESTHER

JUDITH

DANIEL

EZRA / NEHEMIAH

Ruth

CERTAINLY it makes more sense to imagine that *Ruth* was written by a woman than a man, although I have less literary evidence for it here than I do for *Jonah, Lamentations,* and *Judith.* Written by one of the court poets in the century following Solomon's reign, it was still not unusual for an educated woman to practice the inspirational art of writing. In earlier times, Hebraic women were renowned for having been the great poets of legend, such as Deborah, Abigail, and Hulda.

The subject of this poetic tale concerns a woman's position in both family and national history. I'm convinced that it was originally written as a poem when I hear the vestigial elements of poetic parallelism, together with a rhythm of key images and word patterns.

Ruth's vulnerability provides emotional drama throughout the book, especially in her relationship with Boaz. The drama is made explicit on the threshing floor, in the tension between restrained description and high risk. Perpetuation of a nation is metaphorically in the balance; and at the time of writing, both risk and restraint were uppermost in the nation's mind. The symbolic act of uncovering Boaz's legs (literally "feet," though that word does not convey the proper note of apprehension, since there is a Hebrew connotation of male genitals) until he wakes of his own accord, is paralleled later in the ritual act of rejection by the closest kin-redeemer. That man takes off his sandal to symbolize his renunciation, rejecting the risk—or position of vulnerability.

Boaz takes the risk of winning the blessing: "this name will not disappear." And that name links up the line of descent down to David, confirming the right to live in the land. The union with the land is that of Boaz's union with Ruth, primordial native stock. Their child in Bethlehem, who will become the grandfather of David, is thereby a harvest of love. In the words of the vestigial chorus—the women of the city—"the Lord be blessed/ whose kindness has not ceased/ to this day, never leaving you/ bereft of a redeemer." The word "redeem," here and elsewhere, weaves together the contractual ethics in all relationships, from property dealings to personal and family relations.

This contract, or convenant, requires a physical embrace, so that the men are equally in need of redemption in a woman's arms; after all, it was "Rachel and Leah/ who built the house in Israel." In the same way, the reader is brought into the circle of witnesses represented by those at the "trial" and then the betrothal of Boaz and Ruth—"today, in this assembly/ you are witnesses." The risk and the blessing reside in a union of equals, and they maintain it by their acceptance of vulnerability, or intimacy. As in *Esther,* that vulnerability is sometimes a curse, more often a blessing. It is in the intimacies of poetry, the author also implies, that we become witnesses.

❀❧ *Ruth* ❧❀

CHAPTER 1

And it was back in the Days of Judges
when the law was not always lived
as the judges received it
and it was a time of famine
ravaging the land

There was a man, then
of Bethlehem, in Judah, who left
wandering to foreign soil, in Moab
with his wife and two sons—
this man was named Elimelech
and his wife, Naomi
and two sons, Mahlon and Kilyon
and they were Ephraimites, established Bethlehem Jews

They reached the fertile land in Moab
sojourning, then settling there
Elimelech, the man who had been husband
to Naomi, died, and she was left there
but stayed on, with her two sons

The sons settled down in Moab
each marrying a Moabite woman
one was named Orpah
and the second, Ruth
and for ten years they lived on there

But the two sons, Mahlon and Kilyon
also died, and Naomi was left there
without husband, without children

The woman, with her daughters-in-law
resolved to leave
to return from the fields of Moab—
it was there in Moab she had heard
how the Lord took care of his people again
and they had their share of bread

So she left that place
setting out with her two daughters-in-law
on the road that returns
to the land of Judah

Then Naomi stopped—
saying to them
you must go back, both of you
return to the house of your mother
may the Lord be kind to you
as you were kind to our dead
as you remained loving to me
and may the Lord take care of you
giving you a home of kindness
in the house of a loving husband

Naomi kissed them
and they broke out crying
protesting: no, we will return
with you, to your people

But she answered: return, my daughters
why go with me?
are there yet more sons in my womb
who would be husbands to you?

Return, my daughters, go your way
I am too old for husbands, because
if I said there is still hope

that even tonight I had a husband
that even now I was bearing sons
would you wait for them to grow up
would you stay home, waiting
shutting yourselves off
from husbands?

No, my daughters, it would be
even more bitter for me than you
knowing the Lord is against me
his hand already has shown my way

Yet they protested again, crying
and Orpah kissed her mother-in-law
in parting
but Ruth clung to her

Look, Naomi was saying, your sister-in-law returns
to her people, to her gods
return with her
but Ruth protested: don't push me away
or urge me to turn away
from you

Wherever you must go
I will go with you
wherever you must stay
I will stay with you
your people are my people
your God my God
wherever you must die
there too I will be buried

Let the Lord take me—if he must
no matter how hard it is

may nothing but that, death
separate us

Naomi could see Ruth's determination
to go with her
she stopped speaking, no longer
trying to dissuade her
the two of them walked on
together
until they reached Bethlehem

And in Bethlehem they found
the town struck with amazement
and interest in them, with the women saying
is this Naomi?
do not call me Naomi (pleasantness)
call me Mara (bitterness)
as it pleases Almighty God

I was full of life when I left
but I return empty-handed
on the bitter road the Lord provides me
why call me Naomi
you can see the Lord was hard
a stone in my pleasant way
Almighty God was pleased to point me away
from a good life, to futility

And so Naomi returned
and with her, Ruth the Moabite
her daughter-in-law
leaving the fields of Moab
arriving in Bethlehem at a time
of harvest—the barley harvest had begun.

CHAPTER 2

And Naomi had a relative there
an in-law
a man of character
from the established family of Elimelech
and his name was Boaz

Ruth, the woman of Moab, was saying
to Naomi: I am going
to the fields, so I may glean
the free grain that falls
behind, if one may
look on me kindly—
and she was reassured: go, my daughter

There, in the fields, gleaning
behind the harvesters, she found herself
by accident
in just that part of the fields
belonging to Boaz, from the family of Elimelech

And it happened Boaz came out
from the town, Bethlehem
greeting the harvesters: the Lord
be with you, and they greeted him
the Lord be kind to you

Boaz turned to his man
overseeing the harvesters
who is that young woman
and the young man replied
she is the Moabite woman, who returned

with Naomi from the fields of Moab
she made up her mind to glean
behind the harvesters, and there she's been
on her feet since morning
with hardly a moment's shade

And Boaz turned to Ruth
listen, my daughter
you will not have to glean
in other fields
you will not have to leave again
cling to us, stay here
with our young women

Your eyes will be on the harvest
along with the others—don't stand back
but go with them, I've asked
the young men not to treat you harshly
and when you're thirsty, walk over
to the canteens the young men have brought

She was overcome with gratitude
bowing her face to the earth
in a gesture of humility, then saying
why am I special in your eyes
why are you so kind
that I stand out as anything more
than a foreigner?

Because I learned more
Boaz was saying, for all to hear
how you cared for your mother-in-law
after your husband's death
and then left behind you

mother, father, and land
to come to a strange country
trusting in a people you didn't yet know

The Lord be a full guarantee
for your loving-kindness
the God of Israel reward you fully
with a rich life
as you have awarded us
your full trust
beneath his sheltering wing

May I live up to your kindness
Ruth was saying
and to the reassurance in your voice and eyes
my heart is stirred, as if
I were one of your workers
though I'm not worthy as one of them

When it was time for the meal
Boaz said to her: sit here
share our bread and wine
Ruth sat among the workers
and he filled her plate with roasted grain
and she ate her fill, with more left over

As she rose, returning to the gleaning
Boaz told his workers: allow her
to glean anywhere
even among the sheaves
do not embarrass her but
leave some fresh stalks already harvested
for her, let her glean among them
do not judge her harshly

And she worked in the field until evening
then beat out the grain
until she had a full bushel of barley
about an ephah
lifting it up to take to the city
to show her mother-in-law
who was surprised
at all she had gleaned, and then
Ruth showed her the extra grain as well
left over from the meal

And her mother-in-law was saying
where did you glean all this?
where did you work today?
where is there one so generous
to take kind notice of you—bless him
so she told her mother-in-law where
she had worked: the man's name
for whom I worked today is Boaz

And Naomi was saying to her daughter-in-law
may the Lord be kind to him
who has not forgotten loving-kindness
shown to the living, and with respect
for the dead—
that man, Naomi continued, is a relative
close enough to be within
our family sphere of redeemers

And Ruth the Moabite replied
he also said I should return
staying close to the young men and women
who work for him, saying: you will stay
until they have finished reaping
and the field is fully harvested

It is a good thing, Naomi was saying
to Ruth, her daughter-in-law, good
that you go with his young women
and not into other fields, where
you could find you are treated harshly

So Ruth stayed close to Boaz's young women
gleaning until the barley was fully harvested
and on through the harvest of wheat
returning afterward to the house
of her mother-in-law, the two
staying on alone.

CHAPTER 3

And Naomi her mother-in-law was saying
my daughter, it is up to me
to help find you sheltering—
a fulfillment, a rewarding security

I have been thinking of Boaz
our relative, whose young women
you worked beside—now listen to me
it is the night he will be winnowing the grain
at the threshing floor, you must
bathe, use perfume, dress
as an attractive woman
and go down there
to the threshing floor
outside the gate

Let it not be known you have come
until he is through
and finished his meal and drink as well

And when he lies down, then
notice the place—
you will go in and there
while he sleeps
uncover his legs and lie down

And then he will tell you
what you must do
Ruth answered: I will
do all that you say

She went down to the threshing floor
doing as her mother-in-law asked

Boaz ate and drank to his content
his heart full, the work fulfilled
and he went to lie down
at the far end, behind
the freshly piled grain

She went there, coming softly
she uncovered his legs
quietly, she lay down

And then in the middle of the night
the man shivered, turned in his sleep—
suddenly, groping about, he felt
a body laying next to him, a woman

Who are you, he was saying
I am Ruth, your handmaid
spread the wing of your robe
over me
as a marriage pledge
and shelter your handmaid

For you are a redeemer
to me

He answered: and you are a blessing
before the Lord, my daughter
you have made a fresh espousal
of loving-kindness, as you did at first
for Naomi—and this a greater pledge
as you stayed true to your journey
not turning, even to the young men
desirable whether rich or poor

Now, my daughter, you will not worry—
whatever you say I must do
will be done
everyone, those who come
to the gate of my people, knows
you are a woman of character

Now it is true, also
I can be kin-redeemer to you
but there is another, even closer
than I

Stay here for the night
when morning comes
we will see if he honors
his role as kin-redeemer
but if he turns from his right
I will stay true
redeeming you

—As true as the Lord
lives in our hearts—
and now lie down
until the morning

And she lay next to him until morning
rising before daybreak, before one could know
one person from another—
let it not be harshly judged
he had said, that the woman came
to the threshing floor

Take off the shawl around you
he was saying, give it to me

And she held it out
as he poured six measures of barley
then fixed it to her back

He went inside the city
as Ruth returned to her mother-in-law
who was waiting
what has become of you, my daughter?

She told her everything
the man had done to her
six measures of barley he gave me
saying: you must not return empty-handed
to your mother-in-law

Sit down, my daughter, until you know
how it will all turn out
the man will not rest one moment
until all is settled
this very day.

CHAPTER 4

And Boaz had gone up to the gate
where the people gather
and sat down in the square
just then the very kin-redeemer
he had spoken of
passed by: stop, you so-and-so
come over here and sit down
and he did

Then Boaz called ten of the city's elders
to come over and sit down
in the role of witnesses
and they did

He turned to the kin-redeemer:
the part of the field
that was like a brother's, Elimelech's
must properly be sold by Naomi
who has returned
from the fields of Moab
I pledged to make it known to you
it is your right: you may buy it
in the presence of our people's elders
in front of those seated here

If you will honor your role
as redeemer, do it
and if it is not to be redeemed
tell me and make it known
since there is no one else but you
to do it, and I after you
he answered: I will redeem

Boaz continued: on the day you buy
the field from Naomi, you buy as well
from Ruth, the Moabite
who is the widow, the role
of redeeming husband—
to renew the name of the dead
by her hand
and to raise children
establishing his inheritance
the kin-redeemer answered: I cannot redeem

Redeeming may harm my own inheritance—
why not take on the role yourself
the right is yours
I cannot redeem it

Now this is how it was done
in Israel in those days
in cases of transferring rights:
as a sign of validation
in all such things
the man took off his sandal
and gave it to the neighbor
and thus the thing was sealed

Buy it, said the kin-redeemer
to Boaz, and he took off
his sandal

Then Boaz, turning to the elders
and in the presence of his people
said: you are witnesses
that on this day
I am buying from Naomi's hand
what was Elimelech's
what was his sons', Kilyon's and Mahlon's

And foremost, I take on the right
to ask the hand of Ruth
the Moabite, widow of Mahlon
whom I will marry
renewing the name of the dead
establishing his inheritance—
this name will not disappear

And it will live in his family
and in the assembly of his people
at the gate of his city—
today, in this assembly
you are witnesses

Then the people standing at the gate
and the seated elders
said: we are witnesses
may the Lord make this woman
who comes into your house
fruitful as were Rachel and Leah
who built the house of Israel

May your character reflect on Ephraim
your name live on in Bethlehem
your house grow as that of Peretz:
as he was born to Tamar and Judah
may the Lord give to you
and this young woman
a seed that flourishes

So Boaz was pledged to Ruth
she became his wife
and he came into her

She conceived
and gave birth to a son

as the Lord gave to them
a love that was fruitful

Then the women of the city
were saying to Naomi
the Lord be blessed
whose kindness has not ceased
to this day, never leaving you
bereft of a redeemer

May his name live on
in Israel

He will renew your spirit
and nourish your old age
because he is born to the loving
daughter-in-law
who came beside you
and who has borne you more kindness
then seven sons

Then Naomi took the boy
held it to her breast
and she became
like a nurse to him—
the women of the neighborhood
gave it a name, exclaiming
a son is born to Naomi

The name they gave him was Oved
he was the father of Jesse
who was the father
of David

Now these are the generations
descending from Peretz

Peretz and his wife gave birth to Hetzron
he to Ram, he to Amminidab
he to Nahson, he to Salmah
he to Boaz, he to Oved

Oved and his wife gave birth to Jesse
and he to David.

Esther

THE MOST misread poetical tale, *Esther* was probably composed in the second century B.C., when there was a new burst of biblical imagination. The poet used three older sources—one about Mordecai, another about Queen Vashti, and the last concerning Esther—each in a different genre, from satire to heroic tale. The surface of the book is deceptively primitive; its collage of scenes is dazzlingly cinematic, allowing a range of ironies from expressionistic to deadpan. Aside from the plot, the book itself is *about* plotting.

I've chosen to translate portions of the poetry that suggest the terror of vulnerability, allowing the giddy relief of satire that follows deliverance. The relationship between intimacy and vulnerability is represented in ways that echo *Ruth* and *Judith.* The author is likely a contemporary of the poet of *Judith,* and her work may have been a model for his.

The terrifying words of Haman and Ahasuerus (in their banality) permit the magnitude of deliverance to parallel the Exodus from Egypt. There is a striking contrast between slavery in Egypt and the vulnerability of assimilation in Persia (as there is between Egypt and a vulnerable Judean state, in *Judith*). What do the Jews seem to want? Apparently, to maintain the sensibility of their vulnerability. Ahasuerus asks Esther (who has attained the pinnacle of power in Persia as Joseph in Egypt and Daniel in Babylon had before her) what she would now have, up to half the kingdom. In the most poignant understatement, Esther replies (her opening words echoing the false humility of Haman): "and if your majesty pleases/ grant me my life/ it is my petition/ and my people's life/ it is my request—/ we wish to live."

The satire in the book fitted the Jewish festival of Purim; by late Talmudic times it was suggested that one be drunk enough on this occasion to listen to a reading of the *Scroll of Esther* and be unable to distinguish between "bless Mordecai" and "curse Haman."

❧ Esther ❧

Ahasuerus ruled a Persian empire of 127 provinces. He made a great festival for representatives from all of them, lasting half a year. Then he threw open the palace for the common people of the capital city, Shushan, for another seven days of feasting and drinking. Drunk and enraged by an imagined slight from Vashti, his queen, Ahasuerus heeds the suggestion of his councilors that she be deposed. The issuing of a decree, to be sent to all the provinces, cites this action as an example to all males of vigilant dominance. It is a rather comic decree, especially in its bureaucratic formulation, but the process sets the precedent for a later one, in which the prime minister, Haman, suggests the Jews be murdered.

    A new queen must be chosen. Virgins from each of the provinces are brought to the capital. Esther, adopted daughter of Mordecai, is among the chosen. Both are fourth-generation, Diaspora Jews, dating from the Babylonian exile. Esther undergoes a twelve-month beauty treatment, as required in the king's harem, then is brought to the king and wins his favor. Mordecai, who remains close to her as an official in the palace government, has advised Esther not to reveal her Jewish origin. Subsequently, she is made queen. During Esther's coronation feast, Mordecai learns of a court plot on the king's life, tells it to Queen Esther, and so he, too, wins favor when the plotters are caught. The stage is set for Haman.

CHAPTER 3

Not long after these things
King Ahasuerus appointed Haman
prime minister

so Haman, son of Hammedatha, the Amalekite
(remember the cruelty of Amalek)
was raised to the highest seat

among the high officials at court
and all the courtiers had to bow
right down to the ground for him

for this was the king's command
yet Mordecai didn't bow
let alone kneel to the ground

the officials at the King's Gate
asked Mordecai: how can you ignore
the king's commandment?

and this continued day after day
the courtiers reminding him
and he ignoring them

explaining that he was a Jew
words so striking and upright
these men exposed him to Haman

to see if Mordecai would stand
by his word
and be allowed to

and when Haman saw for himself
how he would not kneel
a rage swelled in him

that killing Mordecai could not satisfy
a deep contempt for this man's people
now that he was faced with them

until Haman could think only of how
to wipe out all Jews from his sight—
of whom Mordecai was one—

every last one
scattered across the vast kingdom
ruled by Ahasuerus

In the first month, Nisan
in the twelfth year of King Ahasuerus
they cast lots

or *purim*—as they were known
in the presence of Haman
who was looking for the day

of days, the month of months
which fell
in the twelfth month: Adar

There is a certain people
Haman was saying to Ahasuerus
scattered yet unassimilated

among the diverse nations of your empire
honoring different laws
from those of their hosts

refusing to honor
even the king's laws—
as long as they live

it demeans the king—
so if your majesty pleases
it would be in his best interest

and the state's
to issue a decree for their destruction
and expropriate all their assets

and I will raise several million in silver
for the king's treasury
to satisfy all involved

the king removed his ring
giving the royal signet
to Haman

son of Hammedatha
the Amalekite
the enemy of the Jews

the silver is yours to raise
the king was saying
and so the people are yours

if you please:
do what is right
in your eyes

Now in the first month, the thirteenth day—Passover eve
the king's scribes were assembled
and all that Haman ordered

was written down and addressed
to the king's ministers
to the governors of each province

and to the leaders of every people
each written in his own language
and each province in its own script

it was decreed in the name of King Ahasuerus
and it was sealed
with the king's ring

the letters were sent out
in the hands of couriers
to all the provinces, saying

the Jews must be destroyed
wiped out
you will round up the young with the old

little children with the women
and kill them
in one day of extermination

beginning on the thirteenth day
of the twelfth month
Adar

and everything they own
belongs to the executioner
loot it for yourselves

this document was to be published
as a decree—binding as law
in every single province

proclaimed in every tongue
so all would be ready
for the appointed day

the couriers left immediately
on this mission of state
even as the law was being posted

on the walls of the capital, Shushan
and Haman and the king
sat down to banquet

in the palace
but in the city of Shushan
tears and confusion reigned.

C H A P T E R 4 (1 — 3)

When Mordecai learned of these things
he burst out in mourning
crying out, ceaselessly

dressed in black, in bitter grief
he walked out openly
in the midst of the city

in open protest
raising his voice inconsolably
a loud and bitter voice

a fierce protesting
right up to the King's Gate
a great mourning

as the Jews would make
in every province, loudly
throughout the entire empire.

Esther learns of the decree from Mordecai, who asks her to intercede
with the king. But Esther, anxious and distraught, sends word to him

that she can't do it without breaking court protocol and risking her
life.

CHAPTER 4 (1 2 — 1 4)

And when Mordecai heard Esther's plea
he did not hesitate to reply
returning her messenger immediately:

Esther, do not think for a moment
silently within yourself
that within the king's palace you are safer

than any other Jew
but if you persist in silence
in waiting

at a time so crucial as this
the Jews will still be delivered, yes
saved in another way, by another hand

but you and your family will pass away
like a moment of truth turned away from—
for you are only yourself for a reason

and who can know if you were not brought
splendidly into favor in the palace
for a moment like this—of action.

Esther acts, expressing her solidarity with Jews by fasting with them
for three days. She risks her life, and it happens that her weakened state
from fasting inspires the king's generosity, who grants Esther her

petition. Before disclosing what it is, Esther sets the stage by throwing a banquet of her own, to which Haman is also invited.

Meanwhile, Haman has already built a gallows to hang Morde-cai on. But before Haman can reveal Mordecai as a Jew, the king is reminded of Mordecai's favor in having saved his life and orders Haman to honor Mordecai by the same means that Haman had devised for his own honor. So Haman has a foretaste of his down-fall—victimized by the quirks of chance in his own plotting—before he arrives at the queen's banquet.

CHAPTER 7 (1 – 8)

And the king
and Haman came
to drink with Esther the queen

the king again said to Esther—
while they were drinking wine
on this second day of banqueting—

your petition is granted, Queen Esther
even if it means half the kingdom
your request will be fulfilled

and this time Esther responded
if I am worthy in your eyes
of the king's favor

and if your majesty pleases
grant me my life
it is my petition

and my people's life
it is my request—
we wish to live

for we have been sold
I and my people
to be slaughtered

murdered and destroyed
yet I would not have spoken
had I been sold merely

for a servant girl
and my people for slaves
I would not have troubled the king

with news of a plotter
whose hatred outweighs
his concern for your honor

Who is it? the king exclaimed
and speaking to Esther he said
who would dare turn his heart to this

and lay a hand on you—where is he?
An enemy, a plotter! she was saying
no other than this bitter Haman

as he sits before us
and Haman was dumbstruck, confused
before the king and queen

and the king was so enraged
he stalked out from the banqueting
into the palace gardens

and Haman remained, trembling
but making a plea for himself
before Esther the queen

he had seen the king was convinced
and would make up his mind
to punish him

but suddenly the king returned
to the banquet hall
from the palace gardens—

Haman had fallen to his knees
and was now lying prostrate on the couch
where Esther sat

and the king was beside himself:
will he even violate the queen
rape her right here

while I am in the palace?
and the words were barely out
of the king's mouth

when it seemed the hood had already fallen
over Haman's face
like a man about to be hanged.

*In the concluding three chapters, the process of Jewish deliverance is
presented in the most earthly, striking terms. Haman's murderous
contempt will be turned on himself and his family. The end of the
story remains as stylized as the beginning: It's not revenge the Jews
exact of their enemy, but the principle of* la'amad al naphsham—*the
plotter doing* himself in.

It's not just Haman's end that must be resolved, but the whole machinery of state and culture—which was set into motion, disseminating racial prejudice—that has to be halted and reversed. The real drama centers on the future of the Jews, not the fate of Haman.   3 6 9

Esther

Judith

ONE OF THE great narrative poems of ancient Hebrew literature, *Judith* was preserved in the Bible's Apocrypha. Composed by Maccabean poets in the second century B.C., it typically incorporated earlier legendary material. The Hebrew scroll itself became a legend, after it was omitted from the Jewish Bible. It was read in the early synagogues to celebrate the new festival of Hanukkah, but like the books of Maccabees, *Judith* only survived in Judeo-Greek translations (and like them, was reconstructed in Hebrew by Abraham Kahana).

The Christian translations were popular, inspiring many poems and paintings. John Ruskin, in *Mornings in Florence*, characterized Judith as "the mightiest, purest, brightest type of high passion in severe womanhood offered to our human memory."

One of the charges against Jews by early Christians was that their "nationalism was an evil genius" (echoed by George R. Mead, *Fragments of a Faith Forgotten*). In fact, the text of *Judith* makes it clear that the Jews do not look for victory but merely sweet survival: the victory celebration in the book is a literary antidote to the enemy's cruel intentions. It's as obvious a literary exaggeration as the victory over Haman in *Esther*. In similar manner, the popular imagery of war, heroism, and piety is stylized for effect.

Characteristic of biblical poets, when vengeance is invoked it is as an ironic mirror for the attacker's own self-destruction, a hope that he will be trapped in his own destructive plan. Judith's beauty was an instrument of truth allowing the inflated head of Holofernes to fall on its own.

Judith, probably written as poetry, loses much in a prose

translation. Frequent use of biblical quotations and parallels deepens the harmonics. In fact, the narrative is often secondary to the immediate feelings these echoes arouse. Often, the poet plays with a deliberate anachronism, contrasting it with the revitalized Hebrew poetry of her time.

Just as the eleventh chapter of _Daniel_ is probably a work of the Maccabean Age, _Judith_ also portrays its own times in an older historical focus. There are several reasons for this convention. One is the obvious need to disguise contemporary political criticism: the King Nebuchadnezzar of _Judith_ is probably the same Greek-Seleucid Antiochus as in _Daniel._ The customs of "prophetic history" were transparent to contemporary Jews, a source of both satire and inspiration. There is something heady about Judith carrying her cheeses into the pagan camp. True, the woman is keeping kosher, but the irony of the plan is that she will share these salty cheeses with Holofernes, heightening his thirst and hence his eventual drunken stupor. The poet has turned the ponderous nature of the dietary laws inside out. Likewise, the poignancy of the allusion to the rededication (the "hanukkah") of the Temple in chapter four would not be lost on a Maccabean ear.

Judith's rage at Hellenic imperialism is sublimated into her beauty. A representation of Judaism herself ("Judith" means Jewess in Hebrew), she is religious yet acutely oriented to reality. Her physicality, rooted in domestic happiness and communal responsibility, contrasts with the inflated desire of the enemy. Judith's self-respect as a woman in the highest Jewish circles is played against the enemy's regard for her as a sexual object.

Jewish tradition preserved the story of Judith in later, less vital poems. The original poet was probably a highly educated woman, her work at variance with the representation of women in the Greek classics (which she no doubt knew well) as well as some Jewish religious stereotypes. I would compare her poem to Aeschylus' _Agamemnon_ (in the Robert Lowell translation of 1978). Clytemnestra, the queen, murders her husband—"I offer you Agamemnon,/ dead, the work of this right hand"—an act motivated by vengeance. "Oh, deceiving and decoying Agamemnon to my trap/ was work for a woman. I did the thinking." This representation of a woman's mind seems to me clearly a man's work, while the rich mixture of Judith's character—piety and physicality vying for respect—more likely betrays a woman's hand. The two strands unite toward the end and focus upon the women of Israel: they are leading Judith in dance.

❦ Judith ❧

In the twelfth year of Nebuchadnezzar's reign he began to plan a war against the powerful nation of the Medes. When Nebuchadnezzar called on smaller nations to join him as allies they refused, unafraid, sensing his power was overplayed. He was severely embarrassed, and when he later defeated the Medes he planned retribution.

Holofernes, the Assyrian army's commander-in-chief, put together a huge expeditionary force, with over a hundred and twenty thousand foot soldiers alone, and marched out of Nineveh toward Damascus, intent on destroying all resistance. After devastating various nations, leveling towns across Mesopotamia and Arabia, "butchering all who resisted," the Assyrian approaches Damascus.

And he surrounded the Arabs
burning their tents, looting their flocks
then came down into the plain of Damascus
it was during the wheat harvest and he set fire
to the crops, the fields were ablaze
herds destroyed, villages ransacked
and all the young men skewered on the sword

Panic gripped the coast
in Sidon, in Tyre
in Sur, Akko, Jamnia
Ashdod and Ashkelon lived in terror
they sent their highest messengers
begging peace: "We are here as servants
of the great Nebuchadnezzar, to lie at your feet
do with us what you like
the doors of our warehouses stand open
our flocks, our herds are under your command
every farm and field of wheat
lies at your feet

use them as you like
our cities and every citizen in them only wonder
what they can do for you, what's your pleasure"

These were their exact words to Holofernes
then he descended the coast and garrisoned the cities
where he made allies, chose conscripts
and received a hero's welcome
with garlands, tambourines, and dancing in celebration
meanwhile his army set fire to border villages
destroying claims to independent boundaries
he cut down all their groves of sacred trees
demolished all their pagan shrines
defiled every god they'd clung to
so it would be realistic for them to turn
to Nebuchadnezzar as a god
uniting nations under his worldly power
transcending all their local languages

Holofernes approached the plain of Jezreel near Dothan
where Judean mountains begin to be seen
he pitched camp between Geba and Beth Shean
staying there at least a month to regroup
and gather supplies for his army

By now the Jews in Judea had heard about Holofernes
commander-in-chief of the Assyrian army
under King Nebuchadnezzar, and how he dealt with nations
looting their sacred shrines, then leveling them
they were quite scared, near despair for Jerusalem
place of their one God's temple
they had hardly returned from exile
only recently had rededicated the devastated Temple
cleaning the altar, restoring the vessels
reunited in their land

(2:26–28; 3; 4:1–3)

Unlike the surrender pleas of their neighbors, the orders from Jerusa-lem were to occupy the mountaintops and passages, buying time for the protection of Jerusalem. The Jews were in no position to defend their country militarily, but they could hope to appear not worth the trouble of subduing.

When Holofernes heard that Jews had closed the passages to Jerusalem he was astonished. He asked his local allies what gave this people the nerve to resist, and he was told it was faith in their God, demonstrated by a long history of survival.

So Holofernes gave orders to wipe out this people. And the local allies advised a siege of the strategic city guarding the best route to Jerusalem. This way, the strategic mountain positions of the Jews were useless, and the Assyrians wouldn't lose a single soldier in battle.

After thirty-four days, Bethulia ran out of water. People were fainting in the streets. The town council accused the leaders of a grave error in not begging peace like other peoples. They would rather be alive as slaves than watch their children die. As a last resort, one leader appealed for holding out five more days; if nothing changed by then, he would advise surrender.

Judith, beautiful and devout, a widow still in mourning, visited the leaders and accused them differently. Who were they to set a time limit for God? They were actually negating their faith by setting conditions for miracles. But Judith declines to pray for rain when she is asked. When she does pray, in the psalm beginning chapter nine, it is for strength, in a plan of realistic action.

Then Judith kneeled
put her face in the dust
stripped to the sackcloth she wore underneath—
just at the moment the evening incense offering
wafted to the Temple ceiling in Jerusalem—
cupped her face in her hands
and spoke
her words rising outspoken

from her heart to the open sky
an offering, a prayer:

"Lord, God of my fathers
of Simon in whose hand you put a sword
to reward the strangers
who stripped off a young girl's dress to her shame
bared the innocence between her thighs
to her deep confusion
and forced into her womb
raped her in shock
to demean and disgrace her

For you have said in the Torah
this is an outrage
and you allowed these violators to be surprised
in their beds of deceit
the sheets stripped off them
their beds blushing with shame:
stained with their blood

For the lords among these strangers
you allowed equal treatment with their slaves:
slain on their thrones
their servants in their arms
their wives and daughters allowed to be spared:
captured and dispersed

Their possessions fell into the hands
of the sons you loved
for they listened to you
and were outraged
at the demeaning of a sister's blood
they called on you for help
and you listened

Lord, my Lord
now hear this widow's selfless words
you gave shape to the past
and beneath what is happening now
is your supportive hand
you have thought about the future
and those thoughts live as men and women

'Here we are!' they say
your thoughts are alive in the present
and you've cleared paths for them
into the future

Look, here we are, exposed to the Assyrians
parading their well-oiled muscle
preening in the mirrors of their polished shields
bullying the hills with their herds of infantry
vanity worn on their sleeves: tin armor
their spears thrusting forward
their trust in their legs and horses
their pride in the naked tips of their arrows
their hope in thoughts of total domination—
so locked in the embrace of themselves
they can't know you are Lord over all
fierce in your shattering of wars themselves
great armies of the past are dust in your presence
they were lords in their own eyes as they marched on blindly
but there is only one 'Lord'

Lord, crush their violence
break their thoughts to bits in your anger
at their shameless threats of power

They want to force their way into your sanctuary
to cut off the ancient horn on your altar

to strip bare the ark
in which you are held holy
to demean your spirit with swords of tin and iron
to debase your name

Look at the arrogance of their thoughts
cut them off in outrage
bow their heads in shame
sweep a mental sword through their minds

Put your sword in the hand of a widow
give me the presence of mind
to overpower them with pointed speech
in the sheath of an alluring voice
to confuse them with an inner truth
shaping words of steel
to slay 'equally' masters with their slaves
servant and petty lord
while they are inflated by selfish desire
while they are charmed by feminine lips
while they are caught in their self-deception
shatter their pride
disperse their power
by a woman's hand

Your force is not visible in numbers and armor
does not stand at attention before men of war
your power is indivisible and disarms violence
and you are a Lord to the powerless
help to the oppressed
support to the weak, refuge to the humble
a sudden rescue, a saviour to the lost
warmth in the coldest despair
light in the most hopeless eyes

Please hear me, God of my father
Lord of Israel's heritage
Master of the universe, Creator of earth and sky
King of all creation
hear my psalm

Let my words be lies they cannot hear
sharpen my tongue with charm
my lips irresistible
mirroring their inner deceit
which stares back into their surprised faces
as my words cut deep
like a sudden knife
into those with cruel plans
against our heart, against your spirit
and the Temple of your spirit
the mountain of Zion
the house of your children
in Jerusalem, and let the whole nation
all nations
suddenly understand
that you are Lord and God and King
above all force and power

and Israel stands
by your shield."

(Chapter 9)

.   .   .

Judith's prayer was over
she rose from the ground
called to her maid
and in the house removed the sackcloth

and widow's dress, then bathed
in creams and expensive perfumes
and did her hair
crowned with a subtle tiara
and put on her most attractive dress
not worn since her husband Manasseh died
and before that only on joyous occasions—
slender sandals adorned her feet
brightened by jeweled anklets
bracelets and rings on her arms and fingers
earrings and pins and other jewelry
making up such a beautiful picture
that any man or woman's head would turn—
she gave her maid flasks of oil and a skin of wine
fig cakes and dried fruit
a bag filled with barley cakes and roasted grains
cheeses
and loaves of sweetest challah
then carefully wrapped her own dishes
and koshered pottery
also for her maid to carry . . .

They kept walking straight across the valley
until sighted by Assyrian advance troops
who seized Judith, interrogated her
"Where do you come from?
What people do you belong to?
Where are you going?"
"I'm a daughter of Hebrews
but I'm escaping from them
because they are fodder for you
to be devoured as simply as grain in a bowl
I want to be taken to Holofernes your Lord
I can report the truth to him
I want to show him the simplest way

to take over the mountains and approaches
surrounding this country
without losing a single man
subduing it without so much as a bruise"

As these men listened to her well-chosen words
they saw the noble beauty in Judith's face
and (coupled with her directness) they were overwhelmed
by such physical elegance in a woman
"You have saved your life
not hesitating to come directly
into the presence of our lord
you will be taken straight to his tent
and we will announce you to him—
have no fear in your heart
when you are in his presence
because when you tell him what you told us
he will treat you with deep respect"
a detachment of a hundred men escorted the two women

So Judith and her maid came safely
to the tent of Holofernes—
but not without causing a stir in the whole camp
the news was buzzing from tent to tent
and while Judith waited outside the commander's tent
a crowd gathered around her
amazed at her beauty
this was the first they'd seen of an Israelite
and coupled with what they'd heard
they were amazed at the presence of this people
as their curiosity fed on her grace
"Who can despise a people with women like this?"
they were saying
"We'll have to wipe out this entire race
every last one of them

just as we were told to do
because any that survive will probably outwit
just about anyone in the world—
moved simply by the agony of loss
of such grace and beauty
to bring our world to its knees
as surely as a disarmed suitor"

Then Holofernes' personal guards came out
to escort Judith into the tent
where he was resting on his bed
under the fine gauze mosquito-net
that was a precious, royal canopy
purple interwoven with fine strands of gold
studded with emeralds
and many other gems: as stunning as a crown

When Judith was announced he came out
silver lamps carried by servants leading the way
into the front part of the tent
and he saw her standing there and was amazed
at so beautiful a face
she bowed touching her face to the ground
in homage, but his servants quickly lifted her up
"Feel at ease, woman"
Holofernes was saying
"Have no fear in your heart
I've never hurt anyone who made the choice
to serve Nebuchadnezzar, king of this world
I didn't choose to raise a spear
against your people in the hills
they've brought me here themselves
insulting me by taking us lightly
now tell me why you've escaped from them
to join us—but first, be at ease

you have saved your life
take heart, you've found a new life here
free of fear
no one can threaten you tonight or any other night
you'll learn what it is to be at ease in your life
to be an equal and treated as well
as any servant of my Lord, King Nebuchadnezzar . . ."

*Judith's speech before Holofernes, like other untranslated passages in
the following portion, is inferred.*

Judith's words enchanted Holofernes
they were so well-measured
all his attendants were amazed at such wisdom
"There isn't a woman in the whole world
to match this fresh intelligence
lighting up the beauty of her face"
And above the buzzing Holofernes said to her
"God has done well
to bring you in advance of his people
into our hands, strengthening us
so we may bring a just destruction
to those so blind as to take us lightly
having insulted my lord by refusing to kneel—
your God will right their wrongs himself
if you do as you've said
for your words are well-chosen
and you are a beautiful woman
your God shall live and be treated as my god
as you will live in the palace
of King Nebuchadnezzar, so your fame
may spread through the whole world."

• • •

The fourth day after Judith arrived
Holofernes planned a private feast
bypassing the invitations most banquets require
to all the officers, and he called in Bagoas
his head eunuch who was taking charge of Judith
"Talk to the Hebrew woman
persuade her to join us for a feast
it's disgraceful not to know her better
everyone will laugh at us for not courting
such a beautiful woman while she's here"

When Bagoas came to Judith he was all flattery
"Have no fear fair lady
of my lord, and he will be honored
if you will come into his presence
to drink wine and be his guest
at an intimate feast
and be a chosen daughter of Assyria
beginning to live today
like a daughter in the House of Nebuchadnezzar"
Judith was ready with an answer
"And who am I to refuse my lord?
I desire only to be of service
pleasing him will make me happy today
and will always be
something I will cherish until the day I die"

And so she began to dress
in the fine clothes she had brought
in the cosmetics, jewelry and alluring perfume
and in gentle ceremony she sent her maid ahead

to lay the soft fleeces Bagoas lent to her
on the floor in Holofernes' tent
where she would eat and then lean back

When Judith came in and Holofernes saw her
leaning back on her fleeces
his heart was overwhelmed
and his mind filled with desire
lit by a wish to sleep with her
from the first time he saw her
in fact for these four days he'd been searching
for a way to seduce her
and so he was saying "Drink
relax and let yourself go with us"
"I'd love to, my lord
today I've found a reason to live
beyond anything I've dreamed of since I was born"

Facing him, Judith ate and drank
the food her maid had brought and prepared
and Holofernes having accepted her reason
for being true to her God's rituals
was disarmed at her acceptance of him
and so excited at the thought of having her
he drank to his heart's content
until he'd poured out more wine in one night
than he'd drank of anything in a day
since he was born

Now it was getting late and the staff
were leaving, tipsy, but quickly, as if they knew
Bagoas rolled down the outside tent flap
then dismissed the servants
(natural enough since they were exhausted)
and they went straight to sleep

leaving Judith alone with Holofernes
who had wound up sprawling on his bed
his head swimming in wine

Earlier, on the way to the feast
Judith asked her maid not to leave
if dismissed later, but to wait outside the bedroom
just as she did on previous mornings
since now everyone expected her early rising
and going out for ritual prayers
she had even reminded Bagoas and now
all had gone
not a soul important or unimportant
was left in the bedroom
Judith stood by Holofernes' bed
a silent prayer in her heart:

"Lord, my God, source of all power
have mercy on me for what my hands must do
for Jerusalem to be a living example
of trust in your covenant
now is the time to renew our heritage
give my plan life
to surprise the enemies
to bring them to their knees
who've risen up all around us
great herds coming to devour us"

Her hand reached up
for Holofernes' well-honed sword
hanging on the front bedpost
slung there in its jeweled scabbard
then, standing directly over him, swiftly
her left hand seized hold of his hair
"Make me steel, Lord, God of Israel—today"

as with all her strength she struck
at the nape of his neck, fiercely
and again—twice—and she pulled
his head from him
then rolled the severed body from the bed
and tore down the royal canopy
from the bedposts

A moment later she stepped out from the bedroom
and gave the head, wrapped in the canopy, to her maid
who put it in the sack she carried
with all of Judith's food and vessels

The two women walked out together
just as they usually did for prayer
they passed through the camp
walked straight across the valley
climbed the mountain to Bethulia
and approached the city gates.

(10:1–5, 11–23; 11:1–4,
20–23; 12:10–20; 13:1–10)

Chapter fourteen and the beginning of chapter fifteen describe Judith's
reception in Bethulia, the rout of the Assyrians, and the victory
celebration. A subplot is concluded, in which Achior, a neighbor who
respected the Jews, identifies Holofernes' head, then asks to be circum-
cised and is "incorporated in the House of Israel forever." The book
ends with the arrival in Jerusalem, and then a brief description of
Judith's later life and death.

All the women of Israel come out to see her
on the way to Jerusalem
flushed with the victory they shared
of faith over power
grace and daring over brute force

some began a dance in celebration
Judith was carrying palm branches in her arms
passing them to the women around her
they were all garlanding themselves with olive
Judith at the head of the procession
to Jerusalem, leading the women who were dancing
and the men of Israel who were following
dressed in their armor and garlands
songs and psalms from their lips
lightening the feet of the dancers

Then Judith began this psalm of thanksgiving
and all the people joined her, repeating the lines
the psalm of a Jewess echoed by Israel:

Strike a beat for my God with tambourines
ringing cymbals lift a song to the Lord
a new psalm rise from a fresh page of history
inspired with his name
call on him for inspiration
My Lord is the God who crushes war
in the midst of the warmonger's camp

Jerusalem is pitched like a tent
in the camp of Israel
and here he has delivered me
from the grasping hands of my enemy

The Assyrian swarmed over the mountains in the north
with tens of thousands in armor
gleaming in purple and gold
hordes of infantry like rivers
flooding the valleys
an avalanche of horsemen
pouring down on the plains

my borders would be flames he said
my young men skewered on swords
infants flung to the ground
children seized for slaves
and my daughters for whores

But the Lord God has let them be outwitted
with a woman's hand
their hero fell
and not a young man's hand touched him
not the sons of warrior giants
neither a Goliath nor David
but Judith, daughter of Merari
stopped him in his tracks
paralyzed his brutal power
with the beauty of her face

And instead of fame for fleeting glamor
she is held in honor
because she didn't think of herself
but faced disaster head-on
firmly on the open path, God's way

She put aside her widow's dress
to save the honor of the living
those oppressed in Israel
she anointed her face with perfume
bound her hair beneath a delicate headband
and put on attractive linen to lure him
but only to his own undoing
her slender sandal imprisoning his eye
her beauty taking his heart captive
for the sword to cut through his neck

Persians shivered at her boldness
and Medes shuddered in terror

My humble people were suddenly raising their voices
my weak little nation was shouting with joy
while the enemy, shocked, ran off in fear
they panicked as my people danced in the streets
the sons of mere women pierced their lines
mama's boys chased them as they ran
willy-nilly they ran away like brave sons of eunuchs

Their battle lines were erased
like lines in the sand
under the pursuing boots of Israel

I will sing a new psalm to my God
Lord, you are great, you are our glory
your strength so marvelously deep, unconquerable
may all your creation recognize you
because you allowed everything here
to be
you said the word and we're here
and the breath behind it is our air
your spirit breathes the form of all things
it opens our ears
no one can resist your voice
the message of creation is always there

Mountains may fall into the sea
and seas crack open like a broken glass of water
rocks may melt like wax
but for those who live in awe of you
your presence is a steady candle
glowing warmth and a guide to safety
all the burning sacrifices are quickly mere fragrance
all the fat of sacrificial lambs a brief aroma
compared to one person in awe of you
whose strength is always there

All nations who come to destroy my people
beware of justice, you will disappear
your peoples will see a day of judgment
before God, My Lord
but all they will know is the fire in their hearts
sparked by inflated pride
a pain that will always burn there
as they are confined in the room of their minds:
their flesh will be consumed in it
and given to worms.

(15:12–14; 16:1–17)

Daniel

DANIEL was composed by several Maccabean poets in the second century B.C. from sources existing in poems dating back to the Babylonian exile. They were presented as deliberately anachronistic and concealed provocative, contemporary references while transcending the political arena.

Chapter eleven describes the wars within the Greek empire, couched in stylized prophetic shorthand. Containing the awareness that the age of prophecy has passed, this form will come to be called apocalyptic. In the hands of the great Maccabean poets, however, the conscious irony permits parallels, impersonations, and a resonance of the prophetic books, particularly Ezekiel. The figure of Daniel echoes the Suffering Servant allegory in Isaiah, reflecting the transition from the older prophetic sense of a communal remnant of survivors to the later rabbinic sense of individual integrity, or saintliness.

A Hellenized Jew might take *Daniel* for an obscurely mystical work. The Maccabean imagination, on the other hand, would recognize its inspiration as supporting resistance to Hellenistic religion. A few hundred years of history are telescoped into a few stanzas, starting with King Xerxes of Persia during the time of the Babylonian exile and continuing up to Alexander the Great. It is a broad, dramatic literary convention to have the poem come from the mouth of an angel: no Maccabean reader was likely to believe that angels were prophesying history in Babylon. A suspension of disbelief is required, just as would have been necessary for Greek drama when gods and half-gods were speaking.

❧ *Daniel* ❧

And now I will tell you
the truth as it unfolds
beyond the present page—

before the ink can flow from the pen
look: three more kings
succeed each other in Persia

and then a fourth, the richest yet
translating wealth to power
itching to challenge Greece

but there, in Greece, the strongest king
the world has ever seen
arises, doing as he pleases

and as he perches on his world empire
he dies, his kingdom falls
cracks apart

into four pieces like the four winds:
north, south, east, and west
none into the hands of his descendants

and none of his successors can put together
the strength that was his
for it is torn up by the roots

transplanted to yet more petty dynasties
by yet others than these
and mercilessly cultivated . . .

(11:2–4)

This passage describes the advent of Antiochus Epiphanes, who claims the throne of the Asian part of the Greek empire, the Seleucid kingdom. The "prince over people of the covenant" refers to the Jewish province of the Greek empire in Judea.

And then standing in his place
is the unrecognized—ignored
as if he'd been a harmless dolt

who then, when least suspected
scheming behind the scenes
seizes control

all opposition will be swept away
like water jars in a flood
and smashed—even the prince

over people of the covenant
is lost—
and even though his loyal party is small

anyone making peace with him
is drawn into a maelstrom
by a treacherous hand;

in placid, peaceful times
he will storm into the richest provinces
and succeed and be accepted

as if in a dream
all his detractors suddenly paralyzed
a fact his fathers wouldn't dare to dream

so unscrupulous the royal hand
that grabs like a thief
to reward just the loyal bullies

and with all this even he will dream
of conquering more fortress cities
and he will—but only for a while . . .

*King Antiochus Epiphanes has consolidated his rule and has just
fought a successful battle against a Ptolemy, the Egyptian representa-
tive of the Greek empire. Then he will again invade Egypt ("the
South"), but this time he is turned back and vents his frustration on
the Jews. Many of the Jews have become paganized according to his
decrees, but others are strengthened in their resistance by the king's
self-identification with the highest god of the world. (Coins of this
time show Antiochus Epiphanes in the likeness of a Greek god.) This
portion of* Daniel *offers comfort to the persecuted Jews by setting this
king in a historical perspective that reduces him to mortal size. But
he remains an archetypal figure, whether projected back into history
as the Nebuchadnezzar in* Judith, *or projected forward into our own
century as a dictator.*

Then this king of the north
will turn back for home
followed by a long train of riches

now his mind has turned
to the people of the covenant
his heart set against its Temple

he will set his hand against it
as he passes through the land
before returning home

in a while he'll set out again
invading the south
but now the scene has changed

and in the background ships from Kittim: the west
Roman ships
he will be cowed and turn around

and with his mind sunk in rage
he will growl at the people
of the covenant, ravaging the Temple

rewarding the cowards who turn
against their own religion
then he will unleash his forces

to enter the Temple inner sanctuary
desecrate it
demolish the gates

beat and demean the pious there
defile the altar
set up idols

that make one fall to his knees
not in submission, not in humility
but in utter desolation

those who are eager to submit to power
to lick the feet of foreigners
will be soothed and flattered—for a time

they will slander their own heritage
but those who know a God in their hearts
have an inner strength to resist

and they are beacons of conscience
in the midst of flames
some will be burnt at the stake

or pierced or crucified
or thrown into slavery
tortured, maimed, robbed

but they will continue teaching
and be helped by some who are fighting
even those fighting blindly only for themselves

and those who resist with the openness in their hearts
even as they fall their teaching shines
like metal in the fire: refined

and purified and a healing
for the people to rise and continue
even as no end is yet in sight

the king appears to grow stronger
as if magnified in a mirror
free to strut in his own image

flattering himself above the gods
so arrogantly inflated
he sees himself as the highest god

speaking out of such swollen pride
as if his heart was engraved on iron
to last forever

and it will seem so until the wrath
like his life
is exhausted.

(11:28–36)

Ezra/Nehemiah

EZRA WAS a pivotal poet and editor in the sixth or fifth century B.C., one of the first to return to Judea from Persia. Perhaps a century later his works, and those of other poets associated with him, were collected under his name. Nehemiah was a close contemporary of Ezra's and the book that bears his name contains chapters from Ezra—and vice versa. Scholars assume that both books were once part of a larger one.

Nehemiah was a governor in Judea and no doubt established a circle of poets, some of whom would also have come from Ezra's circle. These were poets determined to revive older Hebraic sources, and they were probably responsible for editing *Psalms,* as well as composing many of them.

By the time Nehemiah returned to Judea, most Jews were speaking a Judeo-Aramaic dialect acquired in Babylon. The common people no longer understood the early Hebrew of the Pentateuch, and translations into Aramaic were commissioned. These interpretive translations, made by the Ezra and Nehemiah poets, were the first targumim. The poets themselves, or perhaps Levite interpreters, read them aloud in the earliest synagogues. The portion from *Nehemiah* depicts this process.

Nehemiah pictures Ezra reading from the newly edited Torah scroll, or Pentateuch. It is a description of the festival of Sukkot, the most important days in ancient Israel, which were largely forgotten by the time of exile in the fifth century B.C. It was unlikely that common people studied the Torah in ancient Israel, so that this passage from *Nehemiah* describes the beginning of a process leading to the widespread study popularized by the Pharisees.

The passage from *Ezra* pictures a scene at the dedication of the new altar for the Second Temple. It has been only fifty years since the first Temple was destroyed. Joy was mixed with grief in a typically Jewish brew, capturing the essence of vulnerability.

E Z R A

The workers had built up the foundation
of the Lord's Temple
the original outline was visible again

Cohens (priests) were there in their robes
they blew the trumpets of assembly
Levis were there with cymbals and lyres

as Asaph had been directed
by David, King of Israel
in his day

and they sang back and forth to each other
antiphonally
"Sing praises to the Lord in psalms

so good it is to be singing"
and the refrain:
"His mercy sings through us

to Israel
as it has
and always will"

Then all the people broke out in song
because the house of the Lord
was rising again

but many of the oldest Cohens and Levis
and heads of families
old men who had seen the first house

and who could see it still standing
fixed in their memories—
these men broke out weeping

loudly, openly
as they stood before this house
rising again in their living eyes

many others were shouting joyfully
a great noise was going up
people in the distance could hear it clearly

and they could not tell by their ears
the sound of weeping
from the sound of joy.

(3:10–13)

NEHEMIAH

Raised up on a platform
in full view of everyone
Ezra opened the book

he was standing above them
as everyone rose
when he opened the Torah

and Ezra made a benediction
to the Lord, God above all
and everyone answered amen

amen—with hands stretched to the sky
in a feeling of deep reverence
then bowed their heads

kneeling, until their faces
touched the ground
their lips to dust

and Yeshua, Bani, Shereviah
Yamin, Akkuv, Shabbetai
Hodiah, Maaseiah, Kelitah

Azariah, Yozavad, Hanan
Pelayah, and the Levis
they were the interpreters

so all would understand the tongue
of the Torah, and the people stood
in their places, listening

as the book was read and translated
slowly, distinctly, from morning till noon
with the sense made plain

to be felt and understood
the Lord's Torah
by all the men and women

then I, Nehemiah, as governor
and Ezra the scribe-priest and reader
and the Levites, interpreters to the people

said to them all
this day is a day made holy
to the Lord our God—be at peace

we must not mourn, we must not weep
because everyone was weeping as they listened
to the sweet words of Torah

then Ezra continued: go, celebrate
with a sumptuous meal, a sweet wine
and send a portion to those

who have nothing ready for themselves
for this is a holy day to the Lord
and not for being involved with ourselves

we must not look so burdened with grief
today sadness is forbidden
it is our happiness in the Lord

that gives us our very strength—
and the Levis also were calming the people
saying: calm yourselves, be still

this is a holy day
and not for carrying personal grief
today no sadness is allowed

then the people went home to celebrate
to eat and drink and
distribute portions for everyone

to make a great festival
in the spirit of shared happiness
an unguarded joy

because all had heard and understood
the words openly read to them
and felt their sweetness within

and on the second day
all the heads of families
the priests (Cohens) and teachers (Levis)

gathered before Ezra the scribe
to look more deeply
into the words of the Torah

and there in the Torah they found
written before their eyes
by the hand of Moses—

inspired by the Lord—
that the family of Israel will dwell
in *sukkot* (booths) during the festival

of this month—the Sukkot festival
and when they heard this, together they made
a declaration, to be read in all their cities

not only Jerusalem, saying
go to the mountainside
gather branches of olive and myrtle

leafy palm and boughs of willow
from which to make *sukkot*
as it is written

so the people went out of their cities and towns
to gather them and make the booths
each family made one on their roof

or in their courtyard
or in the courtyard of the Lord's House
in Jerusalem

and in the avenue leading
to the Water Gate, and the avenue
leading to the Ephraim Gate

the whole community that had returned
from exile, returned
to make festival *sukkot* and dwell within

and since this had not been done so lovingly
from the wilderness days of Joshua
to this day (or so it seemed)

there was a great happiness
a deep joy
in living the words they were hearing

and Ezra continued reading from the book
day by day, each festival day
continuing in the Lord's Torah for seven days

and on the eighth day (Shemini Atzeret)
they held a solemn assembly
a closing celebration—as it is written.

(8:5–18)